PRACTICAL GRAMMAR

*For Sister Jo
With much love
Angela Burt, your travelling
companion on a very hot
day in July 1996!*

ANGELA BURT

Heinemann

Heinemann Educational Publishers
A Division of Heinemann Publishers (Oxford) Ltd
Halley Court, Jordan Hill, Oxford OX2 8EJ

Heinemann Educational Books (Nigeria) Ltd
PMB 5205, Ibadan
Heinemann Educational Boleswa
PO Box 10103, Village Post Office, Gaborone, Botswana

FLORENCE PRAGUE PARIS MADRID
ATHENS MELBOURNE JOHANNESBURG
AUCKLAND SINGAPORE TOKYO
PORTSMOUTH (NH) CHICAGO SAO PAULO

© Angela Burt 1994

First published by Heinemann Educational Books in 1994

The right of Angela Burt to be identified as the author of this work has been asserted by her in accordance with the Copyright, Designs and Patents Act 1988.

British Library Cataloguing in Publication Data
A catalogue record for this book is available from the British Library.

Illustrations by George Hollingworth
Design by Sue Clarke
Cover by The Point

ISBN 0 435 983 156

Phototypeset by
PDQ Repro Ltd
Printed and bound in Great Britain by
Clay Ltd., Bungay, Suffolk

94 95 96 97 10 9 8 7 6 5 4 3 2 1

The Publishers would like to thank the following for their permission to use copyright material:

Caribbean Week for extracts from issues Jan 23 – Feb 5, Aug 21 – Sep 3, Feb 6 – 19, 1993; André Deutsch for the extracts from: 'An Enchanted Alley' (from *Cricket in the Road and Other Stories*) and *The Games Were Coming* by Michael Anthony, and *Capitalism and Slavery* by Dr. Eric Williams; Victor Gollancz for the extract from *The Friends* by Rosa Guy; Heinemann Educational Publishers for the extracts from: *Beka Lamb* and *In Times Like These* by Zee Edgell, *A Boy Named Ossie* by Earl McKenzie, and *Heinemann International Students' Dictionary* compiled by Elana Katz and Christina Ruse; William Heinemann Ltd for the extract from *Things Fall Apart* by Chinua Achebe (William Heinemann Ltd, 1958); *London Magazine* for the extract from 'The Signature' by Clyde Hosein from *The Killing of Nelson John*; Maggie Nooeh Literary Agency for the extract from 'To Dah-duh, In Memoriam' by Paule Marshall (copyright 1983), from *Merle and Other Stories*, first published by The Feminist Press, New York, 1983; Penguin Books Ltd for the extracts from *Wide Sargasso Sea* by Jean Rhys; The University of the West Indies for an extract from *Chapters in Caribbean History* by E.V. Goveia.

The publishers have made every effort to trace the copyright holders but if they have inadvertently overlooked any, they will be pleased to make the necessary arrangements at the first opportunity.

Contents

Preface   v
Introduction   vi

Nouns

The four types of noun	1
Spelling plural forms	2
Using the possessive apostrophe	4
Practice with abstract nouns	6
Punctuation of proper nouns	7
Agreement of collective nouns	8
Keeping your style clear and simple	10

Pronouns

The eight types of pronoun	12
Using personal pronouns	13
Using relative pronouns	17
Using interrogative pronouns	19
Using reflexive and emphasising pronouns	19
Using indefinite pronouns	21
Agreement of pronouns and nouns	23

Verbs

What is a verb?	24
Tenses	24
Formation of questions	32
Formation of negatives	33
The correct sequence of tenses	34
Agreement: subject and verb	36
Using infinitives	37
Avoiding split infinitives	40

Using participles	42
Avoiding misrelated participles	43
Direct and indirect speech	44
Active and passive voice	45

Adverbs

The seven types of adverb	48
Comparison of adverbs	50
Double negatives	51
Correct positioning of 'only'	52

Adjectives

The nine types of adjective	53
Using possessive adjectives	57
Positioning adjectives correctly	57
Comparison of adjectives	59
Using 'fewer' and 'less'	60

Prepositions

What is a preposition?	61
Using the correct preposition	62
Using the right number of prepositions	64
Prepositions and personal pronouns	64
Ending a sentence with a preposition	65

Conjunctions

The two types of conjunction	66
Co-ordinating conjunctions	66
Subordinating conjunctions	68
Sentence construction	71

Answers 75

Index 89

Preface

This is a practical grammar book. It focuses on common grammatical errors and the special areas of difficulty encountered by CXC candidates. Especial emphasis has been given to the use of plural nouns, the correct formation of tenses, the different functions of adverbs and adjectives, and the distinction between possessive adjectives and personal pronouns.

The book is divided into seven chapters dealing with the main parts of speech: nouns, pronouns, verbs, adverbs, adjectives, prepositions and conjunctions. Practice in varied sentence construction, in synthesis and in compression is included in the last chapter.

Wherever possible I have devised exercises that will encourage students to extend their vocabularies. A good dictionary will be useful for reference. I have standardised all exercises with the *Heinemann International Students' Dictionary*.

Grammatical terminology has been kept to a minimum, and I have tried to use language wherever possible that will be familiar to the student. I have drawn on a wide range of Caribbean writing to provide contemporary illustrative material and the text for many of the exercises.

The book is designed for both classroom and individual use. The answers at the back of the book make it possible for students to check their own work.

I hope that as well as being instructive this book will also be enjoyable to use, and that students who work their way carefully through it will speak and write Standard English with greater ease, accuracy and effectiveness.

Angela Burt

Introduction

All the words in our language can be organised into groups according to the work they do. We can call these groups 'parts of speech'. This grammar book is concerned with the seven main parts of speech: nouns, pronouns, verbs, adverbs, adjectives, prepositions and conjunctions.

Our purpose in looking closely at these seven parts of speech is a practical one. By understanding the work that each one does in a sentence, you will be helped to use them correctly.

There will be special attention given to errors that the CXC examiners highlight each year in their official report on the work of candidates. You will be alerted to these problem areas by this symbol in the margin.

There will be practice exercises based on common grammatical errors and practice too in moving from the structures of popular speech to the different conventions of Standard English.

For some of the exercises a good dictionary will help you. You will see this symbol where you may need to refer to a dictionary.

Remember not to write in the book itself but to write your answers in your exercise book.

Nouns

The four types of noun

What do all the words below have in common?

poet	Derek Walcott	happiness	swarm
day	Tuesday	wisdom	anthology
month	February	beauty	batch
island	Monserrat	volume	audience
sea	Atlantic Ocean	weight	flock

They are all **nouns**. They are all names and they can be divided into four categories according to what kind of thing they name:

- **Common nouns** are general names (such as 'poet').
- **Proper nouns** are individual names (such as 'Derek Walcott').
- **Abstract nouns** are names given to concepts, feelings and ideas (such as 'happiness').
- **Collective nouns** are special names for collections and groups (such as 'swarm').

CHECK YOUR UNDERSTANDING

1. Find the 15 **common nouns** in the extract below. The extract comes from *A Boy Named Ossie* by Earl McKenzie.

   He spent the following week preparing to make the fife... He used his father's knife – it was the sharpest in the house – to remove the chosen segment from the rest of the bamboo pole.
   Then, on Saturday evening, while he was cooking dinner for their pig, he heated the nail in the wood-fire and bored the holes.

2. **Proper nouns** begin with capital letters but these initial capitals have been deliberately omitted in this extract borrowed from *Caribbean Week*. Rewrite the extract, restoring the ten missing capital letters.

caribbean cartoonist

trevorne lewis is a 12-year-old student at st michael's school, barbados. A self-taught artist, he has been drawing cartoons for a little more than a year, and he has had some of his work published in the *sunday advocate*. One of his cartoons alludes to the recent controversy in barbados over whether or not flogging with the cat-o'-nine-tails should be reintroduced as a punishment for convicted criminals.

3. Form **abstract nouns** from the words given below. Use your dictionary to help you.

a) poor: po-----y   f) warm: warm--
b) sad: sad----   g) energetic: en----
c) honest: honest–   h) patriotic: patriot---
d) long: l--g--   i) holy: hol-----
e) grateful grat-t---   j) generous: gener--i--

4. To what do these **collective nouns** refer? Use your dictionary, if you wish.

a) constellation   d) flotilla
b) bouquet   e) regiment
c) shoal

Now check your answers with the answers at the back of the book.

Spelling plural forms

The plural forms of nouns can be very tricky. Five useful patterns for forming the plural of singular nouns are given below.

1. Most nouns add **s** in the plural form in Standard English.

Singular	*Plural*
ship	ship**s**
door	door**s**
island	island**s**

2. Nouns that end in a sibilant (a hissing sound) need **es** to be added in the plural form. (You can hear the extra syllable.)

Singular	*Plural*
class	class**es**
fox	fox**es**
wish	wish**es**

3. Nouns ending in **y** in the singular need especial care but if you follow these guidelines you cannot make a mistake. Look at the last two letters.

Vowel + y?		**Consonant + y?**	
Add s		**Change y to i and add es**	
Singular	*Plural*	*Singular*	*Plural*
guy	guy**s**	lady	lad**ies**
monkey	monkey**s**	fly	fl**ies**
boy	boy**s**	opportunity	opportunit**ies**

4. Nouns ending in **o** mostly add **s** in the plural (but there are some important exceptions like tomato**es**).

Singular	*Plural*
piano	piano**s**
studio	studio**s**
photo	photo**s**

5. Nouns ending in **f** and **fe** usually add **s** in the plural (but there are some very important exceptions like kni**ves** and thie**ves**).

Singular	*Plural*
roof	roof**s**
handkerchief	handkerchief**s**
carafe	carafe**s**

Be observant as you read and you will notice other ways in which some nouns form their plural. Some nouns undergo an

Nouns

internal change (man/men, goose/geese); others are the same in the singular and in the plural (bison/bison, sheep/sheep, salmon/salmon). Some foreign words keep their foreign plurals (oasis/oases); others have both an English *and* a foreign plural (syllabus/syllabuses and syllabi).

Creole speakers have to be particularly vigilant when speaking and writing Standard English because nouns which are often not made plural in popular speech need to be made plural in Standard English.

Errors in the use of plurals

CXC examiners regularly comment on errors in the use of the plural forms of nouns. Test your use of plurals. Use a dictionary for reference with irregular forms if you wish.

CHECK YOUR UNDERSTANDING

5. Give the plural form of these nouns. They all follow the patterns outlined above.

a) stitch
b) chief
c) city
d) radio
e) chair

f) giraffe
g) donkey
h) baby
i) quality
j) dress

6. These plurals need additional care. Your dictionary will help you. Form the plurals of these words.

a) wife
b) mouse
c) child
d) potato
e) roof

f) radius
g) brother-in-law
h) woman
i) shelf
j) ox

Now check your answers with the answers at the back of the book.

Using the possessive apostrophe

Standard English requires the use of the possessive apostrophe (where popular speech does not) to indicate ownership.

CXC English Grammar

Standard English: his father**'s** car
(i.e. the car that belongs to his father)
Popular speech: his father car

Notice that **s** is needed with the apostrophe. If the noun does not end with an **s** then one has to be supplied.

There is much confusion about whether the apostrophe should go in front of the **s** or after it in particular words.

my best friend's name
his father's car
the men's voices
my parents' house
the boys' efforts

There is a very simple way of deciding whether it should be **'s** or **s'**. Follow these instructions and let the question sort itself out.

- Identify the owner concerned.

- Put an apostrophe **immediately** after the owner's name.

- Add **s** only if the owner's name doesn't already end with one.

- Name the possession that the owner owns.
    the car of his **father**: his **father's** car
    the voices of the **men**: the **men's** voices
    the house of my **parents**: my **parents'** house

CHECK YOUR UNDERSTANDING

7. Rewrite more concisely in a form requiring an apostrophe.

a) the protests of the workers
b) the toys of my children
c) the bone of the dog
d) the beard of the man
e) the shouts of the crowd
f) the promises of the Government
g) the growls of the dogs
h) the trousers of Mr Jenkins
i) the anger of their teacher
j) the comments of the examiners

Now check your answers with the answers at the back of the book.

Nouns

Practice with abstract nouns

CXC hazards

Candidates at both Basic Proficiency and General Proficiency levels frequently resort to making up their own versions of abstract nouns because they don't know the correct forms.

Prepare for the examinations (and for the world beyond school and college) by aiming to extend and enrich your vocabulary.

Increase your own word power by reading attentively and listening carefully. In addition, take the trouble to check words in your dictionary. A good dictionary is a vital reference tool.

CHECK YOUR UNDERSTANDING

D   8. a) Which word in the advertisement opposite is the abstract noun?
   b) List five more abstract nouns ending with the same syllable as the one in the advertisement.
   c) List five abstract nouns ending in –ness.
   d) List five abstract nouns ending in –ty.
   e) List five abstract nouns ending in –ion.

D   9. Form abstract nouns from these adjectives.

   a) optimistic
   b) cowardly
   c) cheerful
   d) extravagant
   e) beautiful
   f) proud
   g) famous
   h) just
   i) noble
   j) ignorant
   k) sympathetic
   l) critical
   m) sober
   n) free
   o) enthusiastic
   p) envious
   q) brave
   r) cynical
   s) loyal
   t) courageous

CXC English Grammar

> FEEL THE EXCITEMENT!
>
> Wake up to the greatest fruit drinks in the Caribbean.
>
> Four delicious flavours;
> banana
> lemon
> apricot
> strawberry
>
> EXOTIC FRUITS

D

10. Pair the abstract nouns in the left-hand column with their opposites in meaning in the right-hand column.

   a) cruelty   k) apathy
   b) hope   l) pessimism
   c) confidence   m) ease
   d) enthusiasm   n) failure
   e) optimism   o) kindness
   f) simplicity   p) pain
   g) difficulty   q) treachery
   h) success   r) diffidence
   i) pleasure   s) complexity
   j) loyalty   t) despair

Now check your answers with the answers at the back of the book.

Punctuation of proper nouns

Remember that proper nouns always begin with capital letters. Examiners complain that some candidates are careless in their use of capital letters, sometimes using them when they are **not** needed and at other times not using them when they are

Nouns

essential. Their use at the beginning of proper nouns is essential. Take care in writing and check your work at the end.

CHECK YOUR UNDERSTANDING

11. Insert an appropriate **proper noun** in each of the spaces below.

   a) _____ telephoned me last night.
   b) _____ hopes to travel to _____ in _____.
   c) My favourite author is_____ _____.
   d) Our team played superbly in the match on Saturday 14 _____.
   e) The Antiguan reggae group, _____ _____, will play at special performances throughout _____.

Now check your answers with the answers at the back of the book.

Agreement of collective nouns

Agreement between collective nouns and verbs

! CXC hazards

We talk about **an anthology** of poems and about **a batch** of loaves. Be careful to match the singular noun with a singular form of the verb. (There will be further practice with grammatical agreement in the section on verbs.)

   This anthology **is** very moving.
   The whole batch of loaves **has** been burnt.

However, very occasionally a collective noun should be treated as a plural. This is when the context demands that you think of the constituent parts that make up the group rather than the group as a unified whole.

   The team **was** united in wanting to play more matches at home.

(The team is seen as a unified whole. The verb is singular.)

   The team **were** divided over the issue.

(The team here is eleven separate individuals. The verb is plural.)

CXC English Grammar

Most collective nouns exist in a singular and a plural form. For example, you can talk about one specific anthology or discuss twelve different anthologies; you can burn one batch of loaves or you can be very careless and burn twenty-nine batches.

General class terms

There are a few collective nouns which are general class terms and which cannot for this reason be made plural. Some of the class terms are given here:

cutlery (general term for instruments used for eating, such as knives, forks, spoons)
furniture (general term for movable items in a home like beds, chairs, tables)
luggage (general term for bags and cases containing a traveller's possessions)
crockery (general term for china or earthenware vessels and plates)
equipment (general term for things needed for a particular purpose or activity)

As these terms are always used in the singular, never make them plural. Always match with a singular verb.

My luggage **has** been lost.
All the crockery **was** smashed by vandals.
Their furniture **is** beautiful.

CHECK YOUR UNDERSTANDING

12. Choose the correct form of the verb, singular or plural.

a) The entire flock of sheep _____ destroyed in a fire. (was/were)
b) A swarm of bees _____ circling all around his head and shoulders. (was/were).
c) The audience _____ spellbound by her performance. (was/were)
d) The committee _____ unanimous in refusing planning permission. (was/were)
e) A huge shoal of fish _____ spotted moving towards the promontory. (was/were)
f) The jury _____ divided over the verdict. (was/were)

g) The equipment _____ been bought. (has/have)
h) Crowds of students _____ visited the exhibition. (has/have).
i) Packs of wolves _____ been roaming near the encampment. (has/have)
j) His furniture _____ all been destroyed in the fire. (has/have)

Now check your answers with the answers at the back of the book.

Keeping your style clear and simple

We have all been tempted at times to use pompous words and long-winded constructions in the hope that we will impress others with our brilliance. Resist such temptation. Those we most want to impress (including the CXC examiners) will always prefer a clear, simple and direct style.

Language enables us to communicate our thoughts and feelings with precision; the best words are those which serve our purpose most effectively.

The architect, for example, who boasted of designing an office block without 'environment-awareness panels which could prove distracting for the personnel' inspires no confidence as an architect or as a communicator. (He is referring to windows, by the way.)

CHECK YOUR UNDERSTANDING

13. Rewrite these pompous sentences more simply without omitting any of the meaning.

   a) The firemen essayed with assiduity and pertinacity to extinguish the conflagration.
   b) It is necessary for me to effect the termination of your domiciliary abode.
   c) They existed in conjugal felicity in perpetuity.
   d) I proffered my felicitations on his approaching nuptials.
   e) The altercation became exceedingly vituperative and John's endeavours to retain his equanimity proved short-lived.

Now check your answers with the answers at the back of the book.

Pronouns

The eight types of pronoun

> For long moments afterwards Da-duh stared at **me** as if **I** were a creature from Mars, an emissary from some world **she** did not know but **which** intrigued **her** and whose power **she** both felt and feared. Yet **something** about my performance must have pleased **her**. ... Opening the purse, **she** handed **me** a penny. 'Here,' **she** said, half-smiling against her will, 'take **this** to buy **yourself** a sweet at the shop up the road. ...'
>
> Paule Marshall, 'To Da-duh, in Memoriam'

In the extract above, adapted from 'To Da-duh, in Memoriam' by Paule Marshall, all the words printed in bold are pronouns. Pronouns can take the place of nouns whenever you want to save yourself tedious repetition.

There are eight types of pronouns, as you will see from the boxes below.

Personal pronoun	*Relative pronoun*	*Interrogative pronoun*	*Reflexive pronoun*
me	which	who?	yourself
Demonstrative pronoun	*Indefinite pronoun*	*Possessive pronoun*	*Emphasising pronoun*
this	something	mine	yourself

We shall deal very fully with personal pronouns because they cause a great deal of confusion. This is partly because more than half of them have two different forms and you have to know which form to use. Standard English and popular speech are often very different when it comes to the use of personal pronouns.

CXC English Grammar

Using personal pronouns

This table shows how personal pronouns are used in Standard English.

Subject

I am hungry.
You make me laugh.
He is very clever.
She will make a good leader
It is true.
We are working very hard.
You will do very well.

They have refused help.

Object

That dog bit **me**.
Mervyn likes **you** very much.
My parents know **him** well.
The whole class voted for **her**.
His friend didn't believe **it**.
The bus didn't stop for **us**.
Her neighbour wants to meet **you**.
Why not ask **them?**

The personal pronouns in the left-hand column are all **subjects** of their verbs. You can check this by putting the question 'who?' or 'what?' in front of these verbs.

Who is hungry? **I** am.
Who makes me laugh? **You** make me.
Who is very clever? **He** is.
Who will make a good leader? **She** will.
What is true? **It** is.
Who are working very hard? **We** are.
Who will do well? **You** will.
Who have refused to help? **They** have.

The personal pronouns in the right-hand column are all either **objects** of their verbs or **objects** of prepositions. (We shall deal with this again in the chapters on verbs and on prepositions.) You can check whether you need the objective form of the pronoun by putting the question 'whom?' or 'what?' after the verb or after the preposition.

The dog bit **whom**? **Me**.
Mervyn likes **whom** very much? **You**.
My parents know **whom** very well? **Him**.
The whole class voted for **whom**? **Her**.
His friend didn't believe **what**? **It**.
The bus didn't stop for **whom**? **Us**.

Her neighbour wants to meet **whom**? **You**.
Why not ask **whom**? **Them**.

CHECK YOUR UNDERSTANDING

14. Find ten personal pronouns in the extract below from *In Times Like These* by Zee Edgell.

> Seguar...said, 'I know Roger Mais was writing about Jamaica in the 1930s, miss, but our grocery store is in a neighbourhood similar to the one he describes. We all want to help make our neighbourhood better, you know, the drugs, the crime, the poverty. But we can't all be Brother Man, can we? Good intentions are not enough. People need jobs and so on. Don't you think this agreement would encourage more local people to invest in Belize? How about the politicians? Didn't *they* have good intentions when they signed the agreement? And look at the mess, miss.'
>
> 'It's not yet an agreement,' Pavana said.

Now check your answers with the answers at the back of the book.

Popular speech

Popular speech uses pronouns very differently from Standard English.

> **Me** has a problem. (Popular speech)
> **I** have a problem. (Standard English)
> Let **we** go to work. (Popular speech)
> Let **us** go to work. (Standard English)

Moving from popular speech to formal Standard English practice can be very tricky.

The exercise that follows requires you to use the correct Standard English forms of the pronouns. Work through it very carefully, referring back to the table of personal pronouns if you need to.

CHECK YOUR UNDERSTANDING

15. Use the correct form of the personal pronoun to complete these sentences according to the conventions of Standard English.

    a) _____ am feeling very much better today. (I/me)
    b) Both Zek and Marva did all that was possible to help _____. (we/us)
    c) _____ must go to them. (I/me)
    d) _____ do not come from the country. (they/them)
    e) Popo is a man like one of _____. (we/us)
    f) All the neighbours were wondering if Gloria would come back with _____. (he/him)
    g) It is no good trying to guess what the outcome will be. Let _____ wait and see. (we/us)
    h) Something terrible will happen to _____. (he/him)
    i) Is _____ alone up there? (she/her)
    j) Every evening _____ sit on their porch (they/them)
    k) _____ is quite good-looking. (he/him)
    l) Every morning _____ are late for school. (they/them)
    m) _____ took the lamp with great care. (she/her)
    n) Mrs Nicholls told all of _____ to wait quietly until she came back. (we/us)
    o) _____ take so long to reply. (they/them)
    p) _____ sent for the police. (he/him)
    q) I gave _____ a present I would have liked to have kept for myself. (he/him)
    r) Have you ever been taught by _____? (he/him)
    s) _____ know what to do next time. (we/us)
    t) My mother has done a lot for _____. (they/them)

Now check your answers with the answers at the back of the book.

Double subjects and double objects

Take great care with double subjects and double objects.

Nadine and _____ are spending a week in Grenada. (I/me)
My parents are taking Nadine and _____ to Grenada. (I/me)

Pronouns

If you are not sure which form of the pronoun to use, make the situation simpler by dealing with the two people separately.

Nadine is spending a week in Grenada.
I am spending a week in Grenada.
Nadine and I are spending a week in Grenada.

My parents are taking **Nadine** to Grenada.
My parents are taking **me** to Grenada.
My parents are taking **Nadine and me** to Grenada.

CHECK YOUR UNDERSTANDING

16. Use the correct form of the personal pronoun to complete these double subjects and objects.

   a) The captain welcomed my husband and _____ on board. (I/me)
   b) My fiancé and _____ are saving hard. (I/me)
   c) The pupils gave my colleagues and _____ some beautiful cards and presents. (I/me)
   d) Sylvia and _____ were disappointed. (I/me)
   e) Sadly you and _____ will have to think of a different plan. (I/me)
   f) The hurricane terrified my children and _____. (I/me)
   g) Will you have room in your car for my brother and _____? (I/me)
   h) My boss and _____ work well together. (I/me)
   i) Mr Tomlin helped Learie and _____ with our homework. (I/me)
   j) The news delighted my friend and _____. (I/me).

Now check your answers with the answers at the back of the book.

Using relative pronouns

Relative pronouns link statements to the noun or pronoun they refer to. Notice that you can use relative pronouns to combine two short statements into one sentence.

> The man is my godfather. The man came to supper.
> The man **who** came to supper is my godfather.
> The man **that** came to supper is my godfather.

> The woman is my sister. You love the woman.
> The woman **whom** you love is my sister.
> The woman **that** you love is my sister.

(N.B. The relative pronoun 'whom' can often be omitted and its sense retained. For example: The woman you love is my sister.)

> You borrowed a radio. It is broken.
> The radio **which** you borrowed is broken.
> The radio **that** you borrowed is broken.

(N.B. The relative pronouns 'which' and 'that' can also often be omitted and their sense retained. For example: The radio you borrowed is broken.)

You will see that **who** and **whom** refer to people; **which** refers to things. **That** can refer to both people and things.

CHECK YOUR UNDERSTANDING

17. Rewrite these pairs of statements as single sentences using the relative pronouns **who**, **whom**, **which** and **that** as appropriate. Make any minor changes to the wording that are necessary.

    a) José is a friend. I have known him longer than anyone else.
    b) This is the book. I was recommending it to you yesterday.
    c) We met this boy. He was eighteen years old and very good-looking.
    d) I was with my little nephew. I take him everywhere with me.
    e) I want to find a school. It brings out the best in each pupil.

   Now check your answers with the answers at the back of the book.

! CXC hazards

'Who' or 'whom'

There is often confusion about when to use the relative pronoun 'who' and when to use the relative pronoun 'whom'. The easiest way is to break the sentence into its two component statements before deciding whether you need 'who' or 'whom'.

>The person (who? whom?) told me is Mary.
>The person is Mary. **She** told me.
>The person **who** told me is Mary.

Use 'who' to replace subject pronouns: I, he, she, we, they.

>The doctor (who? whom?) you consulted is my uncle.
>The doctor is my uncle. You consulted **him**.
>The doctor **whom** you consulted is my uncle.

Use 'whom' to replace object pronouns: me, him, her, us, them.

CHECK YOUR UNDERSTANDING

18. Use **who**, **whom**, **which** and **that** as appropriate in these sentences.

    a) Vincent is a student _____ works very hard.
    b) The novel _____ I enjoyed most was *The Games Were Coming* by Michael Anthony.
    c) James is not a man _____ one can trust.
    d) The essay _____ you wrote was very good.
    e) The meal _____ I shall cook for you will be unforgettable.
    f) I have just met someone _____ looks like your double.
    g) The car _____ Francis sold us was in a dreadful state.
    h) The rumour _____ Olive heard this morning is true.
    i) Shall I introduce you to the businessman _____ has made more money than anyone else in Martinique this year?
    j) An employee _____ is totally trustworthy is worth his (or her) weight in gold.

Now check your answers with the answers at the back of the book.

CXC English Grammar

Using interrogative pronouns

Who is making that noise?
Whom do you want?

As with relative pronouns, there is confusion sometimes about whether to use **who** or **whom** at the beginning of some questions.

Who is the subjective form; **whom** is the objective form.

A useful way of checking which form you should use is to try answering the question.

Who/whom is making that noise? **He** is.
(**He** is a subjective form of the personal pronoun. You need the subjective form of the interrogative pronoun.)
Who is making that noise?

Who/whom do you want? I want **him**.
(**Him** is an objective form of the personal pronoun. You need the objective form of the interrogative pronoun.)
Whom do you want?

CHECK YOUR UNDERSTANDING

19. **Who** or **whom**?

   a) _____ is your favourite actress?
   b) _____ will be your partner at the graduation ball?
   c) _____ is whispering?
   d) _____ should I believe?
   e) _____ will believe such an unlikely story?
   f) _____ is responsible for this dreadful mess?
   g) _____ will help me tidy up?
   h) _____ knows how to spell 'necessary'?
   i) _____ did you ask to the party?
   j) _____ is coming with me?

Now check your answers with the answers at the back of the book.

Using reflexive and emphasising pronouns

These are the pronouns that end in -self and -selves.

| myself | yourself | himself | herself | itself |
| ourselves | | yourselves | | themselves |

Pronouns

They can correctly be used in two ways only: as **reflexive pronouns** and as **emphasising pronouns**.

> I cut **myself** while shaving. (reflexive)
> I **myself** could never agree with that. (emphasising)

You will see in the first example that the reflexive pronoun refers back to the subject of the sentence (like a boomerang returning to the person who threw it).

The second example shows a quite different use of myself. Here is simply **emphasises** the pronoun I. In fact, you could omit it and the sentence would still make sense; it's not vital to the meaning as a reflexive pronoun is.

Standard English does not permit any other use of -self/-selves pronouns. Don't use them, for instance, instead of personal pronouns.

> ✗ **Myself** is an only child
> ✓ **I** am an only child.

Be careful not to carry over into Standard English forms of popular speech such as **meself**, **heself**, and **themself**.

The only acceptable forms in Standard English are these:

Singular	Plural
my + self	our + selves
your + self	your + selves
him + self	them + selves
her + self	
it + self	

CHECK YOUR UNDERSTANDING

20. Ten of the sentences below contain errors in the use of reflexive or emphasising pronouns. Identify the sentences containing the errors and rewrite them correctly.

CXC English Grammar

a) Aunt Grace gave my brother and myself a surprise present.
b) Meself am an only child.
c) The farmers themselves have often said the same thing.
d) Joyce and myself are going to St John's on Saturday.
e) Heself is always nervous.
f) The cat licked herself lazily in the sunshine.
g) You should pull yourself together.
h) Myself knows the whole story.
i) Sam has hurt heself badly.
j) I saw meself reflected in the shop window and thought how old I looked.
k) Mr Artemus poured himself a drink.
l) Mollie and Thomas scratched themself quite badly climbing through the broken window.
m) Weself saw the two cars crash and rushed to help.
n) Do we ever see ourselves as others see us?
o) James and myself would love to come.

Now check your answers with the answers at the back of the book.

Using indefinite pronouns

Using 'one' or 'you'

Indefinite pronouns, as their name suggests, refer to people in general, unlike personal pronouns which refer to specific individuals.

Anyone can learn to drive.
One never knows when disaster will strike.
You never know when disaster will strike.

Notice that 'you' is an indefinite pronoun when used in this general, vague way.

Take care not to mix 'one' and 'you' in the same sentence.

✔ If **one** is ill, **one** ought to go to bed.
✔ If **you** are ill, **you** ought to go to bed.
✘ If **one** is ill, **you** ought to go to bed.

'One' is rather pompous. If you decide to use it you'll have to keep it up until the end of your speech or piece of writing. You may find it rather tiresome. 'You' is less formal and is easier to use.

CHECK YOUR UNDERSTANDING

21. Make any necessary alterations in the interests of consistency to the sentences below.

    a) Although one would like to help, there is nothing that you can do.
    b) One should dress formally for an interview, shouldn't you?
    c) One should always do the best he can.
    d) After doing one's best, you must wait to see the results.
    e) It's a situation one dreads but you just have to cope as best you can.

Now check your answers with the answers at the back of the book.

Using 'everyone', 'everybody', 'everything'

Remember that 'everyone', 'everybody' and 'everything' are singular pronouns and that you need a singular form of the verb to accompany them.

> Everyone **hopes** for a miracle.
> Everybody **says** the same thing.
> Everything **is** going to be all right.

CHECK YOUR UNDERSTANDING

22. Supply the appropriate form of the verb to accompany these pronouns.

    a) Everyone _____ very suspicious of his motives. (was/were)
    b) Mrs Princet cleared her throat and said, 'Ladies and gentlemen, everybody here in the hall today _____ our speaker well.' (knows/know)
    c) _____ everyone willing to help? (is/are)
    d) 'I am very sorry,' apologised Mr Chandles, 'but everything _____ been sold.' (has/have)
    e) Cheer up! Everyone _____ very gloomy. (looks/look)

Now check your answers with the answers at the back of the book.

Agreement of pronouns and nouns

Make sure that pronouns match the nouns to which they refer. Don't switch from singular to plural, or from plural to singular.

✗ The **fire engines** were coming. Some of the boys ran to meet **it**.

✔ The **fire engines** were coming. Some of the boys ran to meet **them**.

CHECK YOUR UNDERSTANDING

23. Make any necessary alterations to these sentences to make nouns and pronouns agree.

   a) A neighbour can be a source of great annoyance if they are inconsiderate about the noise they make.

   b) 'As far as the house-buyer is concerned,' said the financial consultant, 'it makes good financial sense to buy the most expensive house they can afford.'

   c) An architect will design you a house according to your specifications whether they admire your taste or not.

   d) A teenager can be subject to self-doubt and intense shyness and they deserve understanding and support.

   e) A mother may be endlessly loving and supportive but you should remember that they need affection and understanding too.

Now check your answers with the answers at the back of the book.

Verbs

What is a verb?

> The boys **ran** across the road.
> Stephen **is** very unhappy.
> Belinda **is becoming** much more confident.
> My brother **kicked** me.
> **Shall** I **burn** all this?
> Eddie **has forgotten** his homework again.
> **Close** the window!

The words in **bold** are all verbs; they all denote actions or states of being. You will probably be familiar with verbs as 'doing words' but you should also remember that verbs like 'to be', 'to appear' and 'to become' are more like 'being words' than 'doing words'.

Verbs are essential in the structure of complete sentences, as you can see in the examples above. Can you see also that verbs help to tell you when the actions take place?

Let us look more closely at this function of verbs and examine what we call the present simple tense and the past simple tense.

Popular speech does not always distinguish, as Standard English does, between present and past tenses. It may help you to read the examples aloud, emphasising the last letters of the tense form:

>   *Present simple*: he work**s**
>   *Past simple*: he work**ed**

Tenses

Tenses indicate when the action of the verb takes place.

Present simple and past simple

The table below shows the present simple and past simple forms of the verb 'to work'.

Present simple	I	**work**	we	**work**
	you	**work**	you	**work**
	he/she/it	**works**	they	**work**
Past simple	I	**worked**	we	**worked**
	you	**worked**	you	**worked**
	he/she/it	**worked**	they	**worked**

CHECK YOUR UNDERSTANDING

24. Change the tenses in these sentences from **present simple** to **past simple**.

   a) The children **laugh** loudly.
   b) Zek **smiles**.
   c) I **walk** unhappily down the road.
   d) You **lift** the parcel with difficulty.
   e) Marlene **receives** the invitation.
   f) It often **happens**.
   g) He **watches** the road carefully.
   h) Marva **listens** in silence.
   i) I **fetch** the water.
   j) My mother **washes** the floor.
   k) Wilson's parents **decorate** the sitting room.
   l) My employer **dismisses** me.
   m) Leo **shoulders** the heavy load.
   n) The twins **load** the cart.

Verbs

o) Your aunt **answers** them.
p) The decision **pleases** all of us.
q) The mathematics teacher always **helps** us.
r) James **kicks** the ball across the road.
s) They **pack** food parcels all day long.
t) We **confess** our part in the plot

25. Change the tenses in these sentences from **past simple** to **present simple**.

a) He **advanced** purposefully across the hall.
b) They **glanced** up.
c) You **coped** very well.
d) The girls **practised** conscientiously for an hour.
e) He **surprised** everyone.
f) Helen **danced** with grace and charm.
g) The adjudicator **awarded** the prize to Tom.
h) The boys **played** cricket all afternoon.
i) We **distributed** the Easter eggs.
j) She **showed** us the photographs.
k) Mrs Jenkins **marked** Ella's homework first.
l) The piano duet **delighted** the audience.
m) They **hoped** to reach the South Pole before November.
n) Marcus **finished** his supper quickly.
o) The old man **grasped** the outstretched hand.
p) Fr Larry **preached** a moving homily.
q) Felix and Emilio **followed** the thief into town.
r) The lovers **embraced** tenderly in the moonlight.
s) Sylvia **saved** all her wages.
t) We **believed** every word of his story.

Now check your answers with the answers at the back of the book.

Most verbs in the past simple tense end in **-ed** but there are some exceptions. A good dictionary will always guide you with these irregular forms.

Look up the verb 'to freeze' in your dictionary. This verb has an irregular past simple form. Your dictionary should give you this information, as well as defining the meaning. With luck, too, you will get plenty of examples of how the verb can be used.

This is the entry in the *Heinemann International Students' Dictionary*.

freeze /fri:z/
▸ verb **freezes, freezing, froze**; has, had etc **frozen 3** [t. or i.] (to cause water etc) to become solid as ice: *The milk has frozen solid.* **4** [t. or i.] (to cause a person etc) to become very cold: *I'm freezing! You can freeze to death in the desert at night.* **5** [i.] (usually *it is freezing, it froze* etc) (of weather) to be very cold. **6** [t. or i.] to preserve (food) by making it very cold: *freeze peas. Oranges do not freeze well.* → DEFROST(1), UNFREEZE(1). **7** [t. or i.] (to cause a person etc) to become still or stiff because of fear: *My blood froze when I heard the door!* **8** [t.] to control (wages, prices, taxes etc) by fixing them at a particular level → UNFREEZE(2). **9** — *up*, to be unable to work because ice is blocking part or all of it: *The pipes froze up.*

CHECK YOUR UNDERSTANDING

D

26. Use your dictionary to check the **past simple** tense of the verbs in brackets at the end of each of these sentences. This is a difficult exercise.

   a) He _____ carefully before answering. (think)
   b) The children _____ across the road. (run)
   c) Eventually, Anna _____ me the truth. (tell)
   d) The farmer's wife _____ all her money at the market. (spend)
   e) The three firemen _____ everyone to safety. (lead)
   f) Basil _____ the ball over the bushes and into the pond. (hit)
   g) Beka and Earl _____ to meet after school. (agree)
   h) I _____ the vase of flowers on the table. (put)
   i) The ruthless killer _____ his victim's throat. (slit)
   j) The newly elected representatives _____ an oath of allegiance. (swear)
   k) The acolyte _____ the candles on the high altar. (light)
   l) The play _____. (begin)
   m) The old woman _____ up slowly from her chair. (get)
   n) The judge _____ his summing-up at the end of the long case very clearly. (give)
   o) Jean _____ soundly for fourteen hours after her ordeal. (sleep)
   p) The inspectors _____ the factory after spending two weeks there. (leave)

Verbs

> q) Ossie _____ across the raging river. (swim)
> r) Gloria _____ the table with great care. (lay)
> s) I _____ my speech very nervously. (begin)
> t) They all _____ hungrily. (eat)

Now check your answers with the answers at the back of the book.

Other tenses

We will now add some other tenses to the present simple and past simple. These are the **present continuous, present emphatic** and **present perfect**, and the **past continuous, past emphatic** and **past perfect**.

Present simple	Present continuous	Present emphatic	Present perfect
I work	I **am working**	I **do work**	I **have worked**
you work	you **are working**	you **do work**	you **have worked**
he/she/it works	he/she/it **is working**	he/she/it **does work**	he/she/it **has worked**
we work	we **are working**	we **do work**	we **have worked**
you work	you **are working**	you **do work**	you **have worked**
they work	they **are working**	they **do work**	they **have worked**

Past simple	Past continuous	Past emphatic	Past perfect
I worked	I **was working**	I **did work**	I **had worked**
you worked	you **were working**	you **did work**	you **had worked**
he/she/it worked	he/she/it **was working**	he/she/it **did work**	he/she/it/ **had worked**
we worked	we **were working**	we **did work**	we **had worked**

28 CXC English Grammar

you worked	you **were working**	you **did work**	you **had worked**
they worked	they **were working**	they **did work**	they **had worked**

Present simple: action takes place at present moment

Present continuous: action is continuing and is not yet finished

Present emphatic: (use sparingly) states forcefully that action is taking place. 'I **do work** hard you know! Don't accuse me of being lazy!'

Present perfect: action started in the past and still continues to the present moment

Past simple: action took place in the past and is finished

Past continuous: action took place over a period of time in the past and is now finished

Past emphatic: (use sparingly) states forcefully that action took place and is now finished. 'I **did** love you once but I don't love you any more! It's all over between us!'

Past perfect: action started in the past and finished before the point in past time under discussion

---

CHECK YOUR UNDERSTANDING

27. Complete these sentences with an appropriate tense of the verb in brackets at the end.

   a) Every morning at eight o'clock, he _____ past my house and I wave to him. (cycle)
   b) My parents _____ hard all their lives and they are looking forward to their retirement. (work)
   c) In our garden we manage to grow most of the vegetables we _____. (need)
   d) Sam's little brother _____ ice-cream so much that he is always asking people to buy him some. (love)

Verbs

e) Her penfriend _____ with her for another three weeks and they are having a wonderful time. (stay)
f) My uncle _____ in Dominica all his life and he won't move away at his age. (live)
g) When Helen returned the video at last, she _____ for keeping it so long. (apologise)
h) His boss _____ to speak to him before he left, but it was six o'clock before she returned to the office. (hope)
i) I really _____ to people blowing cigarette smoke in my face! Don't you? (object)
j) My poor mother _____ the kitchen floor at midnight last night. It took her three hours to get the paint stains off. (scrub)

Now check your answers with the answers at the back of the book.

Emphatic and simple forms

Don't confuse emphatic and simple forms.

Popular speech uses **do**, **does** and **did** very differently from Standard English.

In Standard English, these forms are emphatic and are very powerful expressions of feeling

He **does** like you! (How can I convince you?)
I **did** hope to see you last week. (Now I hope you're thoroughly ashamed of yourself for not calling to see me.)

CHECK YOUR UNDERSTANDING

28. Five of the sentences below require the simple rather than the emphatic form in Standard English. Identify the five sentences concerned, and rewrite them correctly.

a) Them does come from the country and them like living in a large town.
b) That boy does irritate me with his constant interruptions!
c) I do agree with you wholeheartedly that something must be done.
d) 'Sir, I *did* hand my homework in!' Conroy insisted.
e) My neighbours does drive new cars.

f) When Felix saw her, he did fall in love immediately.
g) If he did ask me, I wouldn't know what to say.
h) Do try to write neatly! This essay is almost impossible to read.
i) Anna loves her little stepchildren very much and does read stories to them every night.

Now check your answers with the answers at the back of the book.

Future tense: going to

There are a number of ways of indicating future action in Standard English:

> he **will write**
> he **will be writing**
> he **is about to write**
> he **is going to write**

Notice that this last example uses the present continuous form of 'to go' and the infinitive.

> I **am going to write**
> you **are going to write**
> he/she/it **is going to write**
> we **are going to write**
> you **are going to write**
> they **are going to write**

Standard English: It **will cost** me a fortune.
Standard English: It **is going to cost** me a fortune.
Popular speech: It **go cost** me a fortune.

Verbs **31**

CHECK YOUR UNDERSTANDING

29. Rewrite these sentences in two different ways in Standard English.

Example: It **go make** him stop playing the fool.
1. It **will make** him stop playing the fool.
2. It **is going to make** him stop playing the fool.

a) Her landlord says she go have to move.
b) You go be seeing Frank this evening?
c) Who go mind her children?
d) It go surprise my father when I tell he.
e) I go hire a car when I reach.

Now check your answers with the answers at the back of the book.

Formation of questions

	Statement	Question
Present	**He works** hard **He does work** hard!	**Does he work** hard?
	He is working hard.	**Is he working** hard?
Past	**He worked** hard. **He did work** hard.	**Did he work** hard?
	He was working hard.	**Was he working** hard?
Future	**He will work** hard. **He will be working** hard.	**Will he work** hard? **Will he be working** hard?
	He is about to work hard.	**Is he about to work** hard?
	He is going to work hard.	**Is he going to work** hard?

You will see how questions are inverted statements. The subject and the first little word of the tense form are reversed. If there isn't a little helping word one has to be supplied. (These helping words are called 'auxiliary verbs'.)

He works hard.   **Does** he work hard?
He worked hard.   **Did** he work hard?

The emphatic tone of 'does' and 'did' disappears in the question structure.

CXC English Grammar

Questions can begin with special interrogative words like:
where, **when**, **why**, **how**, **who**, **whom**, **which**. Subject and auxiliary verb are reversed in just the same way as above.

Who **is he**?
Where **will you** be living?
When **did Mr Thomas** arrive?
How **do you** know?
Whom **did he** interview?

Questions in popular speech can be indicated just by a question mark at the end of the sentence.

You see the man?
The girl lazy?
I go home?

Forming questions in Standard English is very much more cumbersome.

Formation of negatives

He works hard.
He **does** not work hard.

He worked hard.
He **did** not work hard.

The present simple and past simple forms require an auxiliary verb to be supplied when they are made negative. Once again, as with the formation of questions, the auxiliary verbs of the present emphatic and past emphatic are used.

CHECK YOUR UNDERSTANDING

30. Change these statements into questions.

    a) Antoinette loves Patrick.
    b) She is driving her father's car.
    c) Anthony's parents don't know that he is lazy.
    d) His mother will cry.
    e) You know him well.
    f) The shopkeepers will protest at the increases.
    g) I did not tell you that I met him at the airport.
    h) They are hoping to move to St Lucia.

i) We have failed.

j) She is your friend.

Now check your answers with the answers at the back of the book.

The correct sequence of tenses

! CXC hazards

Some tenses can be used together in the same sentence and others can't. When CXC examiners comment on candidates' errors in using the correct 'sequence of tenses', they mean that some candidates have jumped from one time-zone to another in a short space of time.

Most of the time you will instinctively choose tenses that harmonise, but these guidelines may help if you are ever in doubt.

Use any tenses in these two columns together.

Present tenses	*Future tenses*
he says	he will work
he is saying	he will be working
he does say	he is about to work
he has said	he is going to work
he has been saying	he will have worked
	he will have been working

- ✔ He **says** that he **will work** all day tomorrow.
- ✔ He **has said** that he **will be working** Monday evenings this month.
- ✔ **Does** he **say** that he **will have been working** harder than anyone else?
- ✔ He **says** that he **has been saying** that for years!

Use any tenses in these two columns together. Notice you are taking a step back in time.

Past tenses	*Future-in-the past tenses*
he said	he would work
he was saying	he would be working
he did say	he would have worked
he had said	he would have been working
he had been saying	
he used to say	

- ✔ He **said** that he **would work** all the next day.

✔ He **had said** that he **would be working** Monday evenings this month.
✔ **Did he say** that he **would have been working** harder than anyone else?
✔ He **said** that he **had been saying** that for years!

CHECK YOUR UNDERSTANDING

31. Rewrite these sentences correctly. All the verbs are in **bold** to help you spot errors in the sequence of tenses.

   a) At times she **felt** as if no-one **cares** about her.
   b) They **exchanged** vows that they **will love** each other for ever.
   c) She **calmed** him down and **learns** his name **was** Derek.
   d) He **kisses** everyone in the family, **collects** his luggage from the hall, and **was** off.
   e) I **called** all the members of the cast together and **tell** them what I **thought**.

32. Complete these sentences with an appropriate form of the verb in brackets.

   a) She **wrote** to say that he _____ and **would not be returning**. (leave)
   b) Everyone in the office **agrees** that she _____ hard and **deserves** to be promoted. (work)
   c) My father **had been hinting** all week that he _____ to give me a special present. (plan)
   d) **Did** you **believe** him when he _____ that his father **was** a millionaire? (say)
   e) I **promise** you that he _____ ever having said that. (regret)

Now check your answers with the answers at the back of the book.

Using 'could have', 'would have' and 'should have' correctly

There are no such forms as '**could of**', '**would of**' or '**should of**'.

When I first started teaching I was very puzzled by this common error in the written work of my students.

Verbs **35**

✘ She **could of** succeeded if she had tried harder.
✔ She **could have** succeeded if she had tried harder.

✘ He **would of** told me if he was going on holiday.
✔ He **would have** told me if he was going on holiday.

✘ You **should of** apologised immediately.
✔ You **should have** apologised immediately.

I eventually discovered how the mistake is caused. Students are trying to spell the sound of the contracted form they use in everyday speech.

She **could've** succeeded.
He **would've** told me.
You **should've** apologised.

Now that you know better, I hope you never make this ugly mistake in your writing.

Agreement: subject and verb

In the chapters on nouns and pronouns, we discussed the importance of matching singular subjects with singular forms of the verb, and plural subjects with plural forms. Remember that you have to match up subjects with an **appropriate** singular or plural form.

✘ **I is** working hard.
✔ **I am** working hard.

✘ **They has** written to me.
✔ **They have** written to me.

CHECK YOUR UNDERSTANDING

33. Rewrite these sentences correctly.

   a) Boyfriends gets jealous.
   b) They feel that you are sometimes lonely and is in need of company.
   c) The attention of the pupils were turned elsewhere.
   d) My friend and I was out on the front porch.
   e) Unfortunately things doesn't always go the way you want them to.

34. Rewrite these sentences correctly.

   a) 'You is a man!' she said proudly.
   b) My sister have five children, you know.
   c) 'I is thinking about you all the time,' Tony said softly.
   d) 'If Reuben come, I am leaving,' she said.
   e) Has you heard the latest rumour?
   f) She have no reason to be cross with you.
   g) Have he mentioned it to you yet?
   h) The children is coming home early today.
   i) He says that all his customers has gone elsewhere.
   j) I is hoping so much to get a job soon.

Now check your answers with the answers in the back of the book.

Using infinitives

Infinitives (with and without the preposition 'to') are the basic form of the verb. If you look up the meaning of the verb in a dictionary, it is the infinitive form of the verb that you will find there in the alphabetically listed entries.

Verbs

Infinitives are complete in themselves. They **never** have endings added to them.

✔ I didn't know what to **believe**.
✘ I didn't know what to **believed**.

Infinitives can form tenses with the help of auxiliary verbs but, once again, infinitives **never** have endings added to them.

✔ We didn't **see** him.
✘ We didn't **seen** him.

CHECK YOUR UNDERSTANDING

35. There are ten infinitives in this extract from *Beka Lamb* by Zee Edgell. Can you find them?

> Rounding the corner of the nuns' residence, she spied Thomasita Ek, her short, stumpy body propped against the tall, wrought iron gate in the shade of a palm tree. She was turning the pages of a book open in her arms. A lump rose in Beka's throat as she observed Thomasita sucking on the tail of her blue-black plait, her circular face solemn. Thomasita's best friend, a girl from her own village in the south, promoted to second form, did not seek Thomasita out very much any more. At Beka's approach along the walk, Thomasita's birdlike eyes, with eyelashes straight as a stick, looked at her sharply as she stated flatly. 'Geometry test this afternoon, bally.'
>   'Sister Virgil didn't warn us!'
>   'Mighty Mouse strikes again, taraaa!' Thomasita said.
>   'Did she ask for me in class, Thomasita?'
>   Thomasita shook her head, then said, 'Do you know the theorems, Beka?'
>   'Some. You?'
>   'Some,' Thomasita replied, giggling as she suggested, 'If you say what you know, I'll say what I know and maybe we can do a quick review.'
>   'Good idea, you start,' Beka replied, as they stepped into Milpa Lane. All the way home, oblivious to the noon-time traffic of impatient cyclists, pushing pedestrians, beeping cars and trucks, braying mules pulling loaded carts, and gangs of heat-maddened men shouting furiously as they spread boiling, stinking tar on the streets, the girls repeated the theorems to each other, pausing every now and then to consult the book when their statements

conflicted, and Beka discovered it was soothing to fix her mind on lines and angles. By the time the girls parted to go their separate ways for lunch, Beka had reached a calmer plateau, and could wave to her mother anxiously looking out for her from the verandah of the house on Cashew Street.

36. Correct these errors in the use of the infinitive.

   a) He wanted to conveyed his sympathy to the bereaved parents.
   b) I heard John said that he was not coming.
   c) She felt her heart began thumping as he entered.
   d) I heard someone called out to me as I went downstairs.
   e) I didn't want to talked to anyone.

37. Give the infinitive form of the verbs printed in **bold** type below.

   a) Stephen **went** quickly to the counter.
   b) I **thought** that you were out.
   c) Her mother was pleased when Martha **laid** the table without being asked.
   d) Nobody in the class **knew** the answer.
   e) Have you **tried** to explain why you did it?
   f) Robert **caught** the ball effortlessly.
   g) It **was** too late.
   h) The residents **fought** a long battle to get the rents reduced.
   i) My little brother **swam** ten lengths yesterday.
   j) We **felt** so foolish when we realised what had happened.

38. Match up these infinitives with their definitions overleaf.

   a) to slander
   b) to meditate
   c) to exhale
   d) to mediate
   e) to resuscitate
   f) to excise
   g) to libel
   h) to distinguish
   i) to defer
   j) to adjudicate
   k) to facilitate
   l) to extinguish
   m) to pontificate
   n) to prevaricate
   o) to corroborate
   p) to provoke
   q) to commemorate
   r) to reconcile
   s) to terminate
   t) to waive

Verbs 39

1. to revive, especially from collapse or unconsciousness
2. to cut out or cut off
3. to confirm or support evidence
4. to put out or bring to an end
5. to speak or act evasively
6. to make easier
7. to judge or settle a dispute
8. to speak pompously or with an exaggerated air of authority
9. to reflect or think deeply or seriously
10. to recognise as being distinct or different; to make different and set apart
11. to stir or stimulate to action, emotion, etc.
12. to delay intentionally; to give way or yield to authority of another
13. to bring or come into a state of harmony and agreement
14. to write a false statement about someone
15. to honour the memory of something, especially by a ceremony or celebration
16. to speak falsely about someone
17. to end
18. to bring about an agreement between opposite sides by acting as a go-between
19. to give up or not insist on
20. to breathe out or give off

Now check your answers with the answers at the back of the book.

Avoiding split infinitives

A split infinitive is considered by some experts to be grammatically very clumsy.

An infinitive is said to be 'split' when the two words which form the infinitive are separated by a word or by a number of words. These words in nearly every case can be moved elsewhere in the sentence.

You may decide that you are justified on particular occasions in splitting the infinitive because you gain the emphasis you want or because the sentence sounds better that way. There is a split infinitive in:

To boldly go where no man has gone before.

Do you prefer:

To go boldly where no man has gone before.
Boldly to go where no man has gone before.

CHECK YOUR UNDERSTANDING

39. Rewrite these sentences so that the infinitives are not 'split'. Which version do you prefer? Why?

   a) Try to quickly sort through the file before he comes.
   b) I've never been a person to endlessly complain and accuse others of negligence.
   c) The compère decided to immediately announce the closing number.
   d) Simon should promise to carefully listen to professional advice before taking further action.
   e) We want to most humbly apologise for the trouble we have caused you.

Now check your answers with the answers at the back of the book.

Verbs

Using participles

Participles are used in two ways:

1. to help form tenses

   I am **listening** (present participle)
   I have **listened** (past participle)

2. as verbal adjectives

   Staggering from the **blazing** house, he collapsed on the pavement.
   Dazzled by the bright lights, the pedestrian did not move.

It is easy to form participles in most cases. Needless to say it is the irregular forms and spellings which will cause you trouble.

Remember that your dictionary will help with irregular forms.

Straightforward verbs, as you can see from the examples above, add **–ing** to the infinitive to form the present participle and **–ed** to the infinitive to form the past participle.

    to watch   I am _____? **watching**
                                  I have _____? **watched**

Take care with the spelling. Some modifications may be needed.

    to love   I am _____? **loving**
                                I have_____? **loved**
    to fit   I am_____? **fitting**
                                I have_____? **fitted**

Predictable spelling modifications may not be listed in your dictionary but any irregular forms will be listed.

CHECK YOUR UNDERSTANDING

40. Complete these tenses with the correct form of the participle. Use your dictionary for reference.

    a) The sun had _____. (to rise)
    b) Have you _____ your prize? (to choose)
    c) They are _____ the new road. (to level)
    d) My firm has _____ a lot of business. (to lose)
    e) Your spelling is _____. (to improve)
    f) Your mother feels unwell and she is _____ down. (to lie)
    g) Edwin has _____ the ball! (to catch)

h) We have all _____ about what to do. (to agree)
i) We have _____ you some lunch. (to bring)
j) Mr Madison has _____ all my brothers. (to teach)
k) The children were _____ to get restless. (to begin)
l) She is _____ the table now. (to lay)
m) Everybody has _____ from her advice. (to benefit)
n) The choir has not _____ a new hymn for months. (to sing)
o) The baby was feverish and was _____ noisily. (to breathe)
p) She has _____ to his letter. (to reply)
q) Are you _____ that we should take industrial action? (to propose)
r) The visiting team were fairly _____. (to beat)
s) Our school has _____ the inter-schools trophy. (to win)
t) My mother has _____ my uniform already. (to buy)

Now check your answers with the answers at the back of the book.

Avoiding misrelated participles

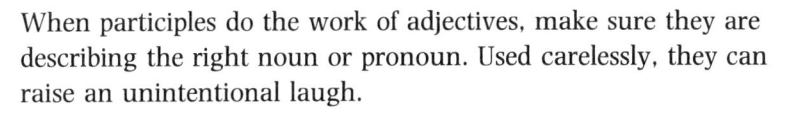

When participles do the work of adjectives, make sure they are describing the right noun or pronoun. Used carelessly, they can raise an unintentional laugh.

✗ Roasted carefully, **my family** loves pork.
✗ Coming round the bend, **my house** is on the left.

In these two cases, it would be best to change the construction.

✔ **My family loves pork when** it is roasted carefully.
✔ **As you come round the bend**, my house is on the left.

CHECK YOUR UNDERSTANDING

41. Rewrite these sentences to remove any possible ambiguity.

   a) Walking home late at night, a car ran her over.
   b) Lifting the bottle to his lips, a wasp stung him on the mouth.
   c) Reaching the summit at last, the view was incredible.
   d) Daintily prepared, everyone should enjoy ackee and saltfish.

Verbs

e) Driven mad by infantile squabbling, the children were sent to bed by their irate father.

Now check your answers with the answers at the back of the book.

Direct and indirect speech

Direct speech: actual words of speaker
Indirect speech: a report of what was said

Both the passages below come from the early pages of *The Games Were Coming* by Michael Anthony.

Can you see how the use of direct speech in the first extract helps us to understand more clearly the relationship between father and son? It supplies us with some significant evidence – the way they talk to each other.

> **'You bring the stop-watch?'** Leon asked.
> **'Yes.'**
> He glanced at his father's face. They were two big, powerful men and the boy was always proud to walk along with his father. The boy wondered if he had spoken harshly when he had spoken a moment ago.
> **'Listen, I want you to give me a good work-out today, see?'**
> **'Sure,'** the father said.

In the second passage, a report of the gist of what was said by the rival cyclists is given. This is all the author needs to convey. To record their conversation in more detail would slow the story down to no purpose.

> They were talking now of **how fast the track was** and **how they hoped it wouldn't crack up for the Southern Games**. And another of them said **this track never cracked up, this was not the Three A's ground in Port of Spain**. They all agreed.

Converting direct speech to indirect speech

This is quite a sophisticated process (it's always much easier to write direct speech) but one that you might like to practise in your own writing and to be aware of in your reading.

CXC English Grammar

- Move tenses back in time.

    'I shall sleep like a log,' he declared.
    He said/declared that he **would sleep** like a log.

- Make any necessary changes to pronouns.

    'I shall sleep like a log,' he declared.
    He said/declared that **he** would sleep like a log.

- Change 'here' and 'now' references to 'there' and 'then'.

    'Come to dinner here tomorrow,' he urged.
    He urged me to come to dinner **there the next day**.

- Use verbs and adverbs to summarise.

    'I really am most terribly sorry and I can't apologise enough,' she said.
    She **apologised profusely/at length**.

CHECK YOUR UNDERSTANDING

42. Rewrite these quotations from Zee Edgell's *In Times Like These* as indirect speech.

    a) 'You have fine-looking children, Pavana,' Mr Grant said, 'and they look exactly like you did at their age.'
    b) 'You'll be surprised, Pavana, at the number of things that have happened here in the week you've been gone,' Jen said.
    c) 'But I love having you all here,' Jackie Lee said.
    d) 'Everything about this job seems to be a problem,' Pavana said, 'but I'll try to find a way.'
    e) 'Eric,' Pavana interrupted, 'and you, too, Lisa. I will discuss it with you tomorrow.'

Now check your answers with the answers at the back of the book.

Active and passive voice

When the subject of the verb is **doing** the action of the verb, the verb is said to be in the active voice.

When the subject of the verb is **suffering** the action of the verb, the verb is said to be in the passive voice.

	Mr Brown	eats	bananas every day.
Active	subject	verb	

Passive |Bananas| |are eaten| every day by Mr Brown.
                    subject   verb

Be alert when you are reading as to whether the active or the passive voice is being used. If you are able to use either with ease, you can make an informed choice in your own writing.

The passive voice can seem long-winded and pompous (in our example above?) but there are occasions when it comes into its own.

> ### CONCERN AS FINANCE MINISTER RESIGNS
> by Michael Becker
> for *Caribbean Week*
>
> KINGSTON, Jamaica – Friday the 13th lived up to its reputation as the government **was forced** to make the embarrassing announcement that its widely respected finance minister, Hugh Small, was resigning.

Can you see that the use of the passive here spotlights the government's predicament – **the government was forced**... – without for the moment explaining how the situation came about and who was responsible for this outcome?

Later in the same article, we have this paragraph:

> In his letter to Prime Minister P. J. Patterson, Mr Small noted there was 'too much uncertainty and delay in the past four weeks while we [Cabinet] debated the new policy measures which **were announced** in my budget speech in June.'

Mr Small could have said, '...while we [Cabinet] debated the new policy measures which **I announced** in my budget speech in June.'

This would change the emphasis and weaken the point he is making about the delay in approving the policy measures.

The choice between using the active or the passive voice depends very much on the emphasis you require in a particular context. Experiment a little when you are drafting your work.

CHECK YOUR UNDERSTANDING

43. Rewrite these sentences using the passive voice.

    a) The hurricane destroyed all the boats in Grenada.
    b) Dr Jagar leads the People's Progressive Party.

c) The Public Accounts Committee has investigated the affairs of the St Joseph Hospital.
d) Osman, Adams and Partners have designed the new building.
e) Tropical Storm Cindy hit Martinique on 15 August.

44. Rewrite these sentences using the active voice.

a) The needs of the disabled have been completely overlooked by the town planners.
b) All the classrooms have been painted by the pupils themselves.
c) The poor child was soundly whipped by his father.
d) The spin attack will be led by Pakistan's 'Bowler of the Year', Nadeem Khan.
e) Already land has been abandoned by some 15 per cent of banana growers.

Now check your answers with the answers at the back of the book.

Adverbs

The seven types of adverb

> But the tension was **rapidly** mounting. British Guiana in 1808, Barbados in 1816. In 1823 British Guiana went **up** in flames, for the second time. Fifty plantations revolted, embracing a population of 12,000. **Here again** the revolt was **so carefully** and **secretly** planned that it took the planters **unawares**. The slaves demanded unconditional emancipation. The governor expostulated with them – they must go **gradually** and **not** be precipitate. The slaves listened **coldly**.

In the extract above from *Capitalism and Slavery* written by the former Prime Minister of Trinidad and Tobago, Dr Eric Williams, all the words in **bold** are adverbs.

Adverbs usually tell us about verbs.

Adverbs of place	(tell us **where**) Come **here**.
Adverbs of time	(tell us **when**) He left **immediately**.
Adverbs of manner	(tell us **how**) They listened **coldly**.
Relative adverbs	(relate to nouns) This is the house **where** I was born.
Interrogative adverbs	(introduce questions) **When** can you start?
Adverbs of negation	(make negative) It is **not** too late.
Adverbs of degree	(relate to adjectives and adverbs) You are **so** kind. I shall accept **very** gratefully.

CHECK YOUR UNDERSTANDING

45. Complete these sentences with the type of adverb indicated in brackets.

   a) _____ have you hidden my pencil-case? (interrogative adverb)

CXC English Grammar

b) He was standing _____ when I last saw him. (adverb of place)
c) The fashion model walked _____ on to the catwalk. (adverb of manner)
d) I was _____ whisked into hospital. (adverb of time)
e) Do _____ forget to check your work for careless errors. (adverb of negation)
f) The child was _____ scared. (adverb of degree)
g) Do you remember the factory _____ he used to work? (relative adverb)
h) The teacher looked _____ at the pupil. (adverb of manner)
i) He spoke _____ calmly but you could tell that he was angry. (adverb of degree)
j) The cat stretched _____ in the sun. (adverb of manner)

46. Adverbs, by giving us additional information, supply precision and colour to what could otherwise be rather dull sentences. Choose vivid **adverbs of manner** to indicate how these actions were performed.

    a) Pearlette looked at him _____.
    b) The clock ticked _____.
    c) The wind blew _____.
    d) The student worked _____.
    e) My mother spoke _____.

47. Form adverbs from these words. Remember that your dictionary will help you.

    Either your dictionary will list all words in the same family together and you can find the adverb that way, or the adverb will be close by alphabetically.

    a) ostentation   f) confidence
    b) aggression   g) ecstasy
    c) vigour   h) affection
    d) apology   i) venom
    e) pessimism   j) chaos

Now check your answers with the answers at the back of the book.

Popular speech

Popular speech may use adjectives where Standard English requires adverbs.

> I know him **good**. (Popular speech)
> I know him **well**. (Standard English)

CHECK YOUR UNDERSTANDING

48. Rewrite these sentences, changing the adjectives shown in **bold** into adverbs.

   a) Talk **gentle** to her. She is very frightened.
   b) The twins are working really **good**.
   c) When I questioned him, Mark answered very **sullen**.
   d) Matthew knew that his uncle was rather deaf and so did his best to speak extra **clear** when he was with him.
   e) I wish I had learned to type **proper** right at the beginning. It's too late to learn to touch-type now.

Now check your answers with the answers at the back of the book.

Comparison of adverbs

Use the **comparative** form when comparing with **one** other.

Use the **superlative** form when comparing with **two or more**.

Most one-syllabled adverbs take –**er** in the comparative and –**est** in the superlative.

> Of the two boys, Winston works hard**er**.
> Of all the boys I've ever taught, he works the hard**est**.

Most of the other adverbs use the words 'more' and 'most'.

> Of the two boys, Winston works **more slowly**.
> Of them all, Winston works **most slowly**.

Be extra careful with these tricky irregular ones.

	Comparative	*Superlative*
well	better	best
badly	worse	worst

CXC English Grammar

	Comparative	Superlative
much	more	most
little	less	least

CHECK YOUR UNDERSTANDING

49. Complete these sentences with the appropriate form of the comparative or superlative.

   a) Sam dances _____ than Michael. (energetically)
   b) They can run _____ than we can. (quickly)
   c) Look at everybody's handwriting and decide who writes _____. (neatly)
   d) Elephants live _____ than tigers. (long)
   e) All the boys were very greedy but Justin ate _____. (much)

Now check your answers with the answers at the back of the book.

Double negatives

I am **not an ungenerous** person.
(= I am a generous person.)

She was **not unaware** of his kindness.
(= She was aware of his kindness.)

Using two negative words as in these two examples is a roundabout way of making a positive statement. There are times when this rather distant, detached tone is appropriate, but be careful. Too many double negatives can be confusing for the reader, and all good writing should aim at clarity.

It is **not uncommon** (= it is common) to find that students have used double negatives unintentionally, not realising that they are saying the very opposite of what they intended.

These double negatives are ungrammatical:

The boy **wasn't hardly** awake.
I **don't** owe you **nothing**.

Correct positioning of 'only'

> ! CXC hazards

'Only' should be placed next to the word to which it refers. This avoids any possible confusion. You can see how powerfully it affects the sense in these examples.

Only Parveen is allowed to read this book this week. (= no one else)

Parveen is allowed **only to read** this book this week. (= she may read it but not photocopy it, etc.)

Parveen is allowed to read **only this book** this week. (= reading restricted to one book)

Parveen is allowed to read this book **only this week**. (= for one week only)

CHECK YOUR UNDERSTANDING

50. Explain the difference in meaning.

   a) Only CXC candidates should queue outside the General Hall at 10 a.m.
   b) CXC candidates should only queue outside the General Hall at 10 a.m.
   c) CXC candidates should queue only outside the General Hall at 10 a.m.
   d) CXC candidates should queue outside the General Hall only at 10 a.m.

51. Explain the difference in meaning between the sentences in these pairs.

   a) She is an only child.
      She is only a child.
   b) Babies can only crawl.
      Only babies can crawl.
   c) I drink only fruit juice.
      Only I drink fruit juice.
   d) You can see her for only five minutes.
      Only you can see her for five minutes.

Check your answers with the answers at the back of the book.

CXC English Grammar

Adjectives

The nine types of adjective

> **This** convent was **my** refuge, a place of sunshine and of death where very early in the morning the clap of a **wooden** signal woke the nine of us who slept in the **long** dormitory. We woke to see Sister Marie Augustine sitting, **serene** and **neat**, bolt **upright** in a **wooden** chair. The **long brown** room was **full** of **gold** sunlight and shadows of trees moving quietly.
>
> Jean Rhys, *Wide Sargasso Sea*

In this extract, taken from 'Wide Sargasso Sea' by Jean Rhys, all the words printed in **bold** are adjectives. Adjectives describe nouns and pronouns.

There are nine kinds of adjectives but most of the adjectives we use are adjectives of quality, describing some quality or characteristic in a noun or pronoun.

There is no need to memorise the terms below but it is useful to recognise the range of work that adjectives do.

Adjectives of quality
She feels **sad**.

Adjectives of quantity (refer to number and amount)
Several members of the audience wept.

Demonstrative adjectives (this, that, these, those)
This pen has been found in the road.

Possessive adjectives (indicate possession)
Anna touched **his** hand.

Interrogative adjectives (introduce questions)
Whose essay is this?

Relative adjectives (link adjectival clauses to words described)

The actress **whose** performance you so much admired is on television tonight.

Emphasising adjectives (emphasise)
You are the **very** person I need.

Exclamatory adjectives (exclaim)
What energy you children have!

Proper adjectives (adjectives formed from proper nouns and therefore needing a capital letter)
He is a **Jamaican** doctor.

Sometimes nouns are used adjectivally:

We shall be staying in a **luxury** hotel.

CHECK YOUR UNDERSTANDING

52. Find the adjectives in these sentences taken from a short story called 'The Signature' by Clyde Hosein. The number of adjectives in each sentence is indicated in brackets at the end.

   a) She gave no immediate reason for her tears. (3)
   b) I vowed to teach her not only to sign Vashti Deen on government forms and my school reports but also to read and write as well as I. (3)
   c) My mother did not think that the old language would help her children survive in the new ways of the modern world. (5)
   d) Now that I tell the story I remember that whenever my mother sat down to practise her signature her face became almost angelic. (4)
   e) She tried to sign her name like an old hand at it, effortlessly, and after a while she did...Practising her signature and counting became an obsession. (3)
   f) I unfold that square of paper many times. I see the inkstained childish hand: Vashti Deen. (4)
   g) I still keep it in my wallet today even though so many years have passed and I am exiled to a far country. (3)

53. Supply vivid adjectives in the sentences below.

   a) The mango was _____ , _____ and _____ .
   b) The old lady's face was very _____ .
   c) The _____ sun beat down upon Adam's back.
   d) The _____ , _____ car stopped, never to go again.

54 CXC English Grammar

e) The puppy gazed at me with _____ , _____ eyes.
f) The bully gave me a _____ punch and I collapsed.

58. Match the adjectives with the definitions. You may, of course, use your dictionary to help you.

a) nostalgic
b) diffident
c) irascible
d) benevolent
e) iridescent
f) meticulous
g) buoyant
h) facetious
i) nonchalant
j) apprehensive
k) evasive

1. having or showing rainbow colours
2. easily angered
3. extremely careful about details
4. of a silly attempt to be amusing
5. unconcerned, cool or indifferent
6. fearful about what may happen
7. avoiding cleverly
8. able to float
9. lacking self-confidence
10. wishing well to others
11. longing for person, places, things which are past or distant

59. Complete

a) C _ L
b) A _ _ Y
c) R _ _ C
d) I _ _ _ D
e) B _ _ _ L
f) B _ _ _ _ E
g) E _ _ _ A N T
h) A _ _ _ _ _ E
i) N _ _ _ _ _ _ I C

a) moderately cold
b) full of anger
c) rural
d) not having official force or effect
e) speaking with excessive pride about oneself
f) eager to fight
g) much too expensive
h) nearly correct or accurate
i) in accordance with nature (esp. in art or literature)

Adjectives

60. Explain the difference in meaning between:

a) uninterested and disinterested
b) childish and childlike
c) catholic and Catholic
d) infectious and contagious
e) eligible and illegible

61. Without repeating yourself, supply the following.

a) five adjectives which describe your clothes
b) five adjectives which describe your character
c) five adjectives which describe your voice
d) five adjectives which describe your handwriting
e) five adjectives which describe your hair

62. Form adjectives from these nouns. Use a dictionary for reference, if you wish.

a) circle   circ-----
b) giant   gi------
c) chaos   chao---
d) ridicule ridic-----
e) expense   expens---

63. Form adjectives from these verbs. Use a dictionary for reference, if you wish.

a) imagine   imag--------
b) decide   deci----
c) moisten   moi--
d) destroy   destr------
e) favour   favour---

Now check your answers with the answers at the back of the book.

56 *CXC English Grammar*

Using possessive adjectives

As we discussed in the chapter on pronouns, it is important to take care not to confuse possessive adjectives with personal pronouns.

my house
your (singular) father
his bicycle
her car
its cover

our apologies
your (plural) families
their children

Popular speech often uses personal pronouns where Standard English would use possessive adjectives.

> I know your mother well and I forgive you for **she** sake.
> (Popular Speech)

> I know your mother well and I forgive you for **her** sake.
> (Standard English)

CHECK YOUR UNDERSTANDING

64. Rewrite, using possessive adjectives where required according to the conventions of Standard English.

a) 'Eat you supper and go straight to bed!' said his mother crossly.
b) Don't drag you feet along the ground like that!
c) The little girl hid behind she mother's skirt.
d) Me father is always tired these days.
e) Have you hurt you arm?
f) They fought on we side in the last war.
g) Me firm ambition is to become a millionaire.
h) Maria folded she arms and waited.
i) Ted ran back to he house.
j) I ask you all to give me you vote next week!

Now check your answers with the answers at the back of the book.

Positioning adjectives correctly

a **three-legged** stool – adjective
a stool **with three legs** – adjectival phrase
a stool **which has three legs** – adjectival clause

Adjectives

Make sure that adjectives, adjectival phrases and adjectival clauses refer to the noun or pronoun intended.

If you position them carelessly, the result can be unintentionally amusing.

✗ Wanted: a stool by advertiser with three legs
✓ Wanted by advertiser: a three-legged stool

CHECK YOUR UNDERSTANDING

65. Rewrite, removing any ambiguity.

a) For sale: vacuum cleaner recently overhauled by mechanic with new hose and dustbag.
b) Arthritic and incontinent, my mother decided sadly that her sixteen-year-old retriever should be put to sleep.
c) Mrs Kelly visited her mother. She is very lonely.
d) I gave the safety-pins to the pupil I always keep in my handbag.
e) She bought bicycles for the children with chrome fittings.

Now check your answers with the answers at the back of the book.

Comparison of adjectives

Some adjectives (but not all adjectives) can be used at different levels of comparison.

Use the **comparative** form when comparing **one** with another.

Use the **superlative** form when comparing one with **two or more**.

Most one-syllabled adjectives take **–er** in the comparative and **–est** in the superlative.

> Emilio is **taller** than Ricardo.
> Tony is the **tallest** boy in the school.

Most of the other adjectives use the words 'more' and 'most'.

> Emilio is **more energetic** than Ricardo.
> Tony is the **most energetic** boy in the school.

If you use 'less' and 'least' you can take adjectives in the opposite direction (down the scale).

> He is **less energetic** than she is.
> Helen is the **least envious** girl I have ever met.

Take care with these two quite irregular adjectives.

	Comparative	Superlative
good	better	best
bad	worse	worst

Take care also not to use absolute adjectives in the comparative and superlative. Words like 'unique', 'perfect', 'excellent', 'complete' and so on are not comparable. Something is either unique or it isn't. You can't have shades of uniqueness.

CHECK YOUR UNDERSTANDING

66. Some of these sentences need adjustment; some are perfectly acceptable. Discuss in pairs which sentences need to be altered.

   a) Rose is the most beautifullest girl I have ever met.
   b) Look at the two of them and tell me which one is tallest.
   c) Michael is the most generous person I have ever known.

d) The less attention you pay her, the sooner she will recover.
e) Simon's legs are longer than yours. It's no wonder that he can walk at a more faster pace.
f) Do you feel you would be more happier at a boarding school?
g) The exhibition of Russian icons in New York was the most magnificent of its kind ever seen.
h) I have just moved to one of the most noisiest villages you can imagine.
i) Carol is slimmer than I remember.
j) It is hotter today than it was yesterday.

Now check your answers with the answers at the back of the book.

Using 'fewer' and 'less'

Use 'fewer' with plural nouns (i.e. nouns that can be counted).

I drink **fewer** cups of coffee these days.
There are **fewer** opportunities for explorers today.

Use 'less' with nouns that cannot be counted (i.e. nouns which are always singular).

I drink **less** coffee now than I used to.
There is **less** scope to use my initiative in this new job.

CHECK YOUR UNDERSTANDING

67. Use **less** or **fewer** in these sentences as appropriate.

a) I smoke _____ cigarettes than you do.
b) There were _____ arrests in Port of Spain last year.
c) You should eat _____ sugar, you know.
d) The President will have _____ authority under the new constitution.
e) There are _____ candidates standing for election this year.

Now check your answers with the answers at the back of the book.

Prepositions

What is a preposition?

> **For** three centuries the Caribbean had been a great centre **of** European rivalry; its islands had been valued not only **for** their produce, but **for** their strategic location. The Caribbean had been both a trading centre **in** its own right and a highway **to** and **from** the riches **of** Mexico and Peru.
>
> The struggle had taken many forms but **by** the late 18th and early 19th century the main conflict had narrowed **to** that **between** Britain and France.
>
> E. V. Goveia, Chapters in Caribbean History

Prepositions show how nouns and pronouns relate to the rest of the sentence. They can indicate position, manner, time, direction, ownership and so on.

> Leave your books **on** your desks. (position)
> They answered **with** quiet dignity. (manner)
> We should make a start **before** breakfast. (time)
> Which is the best road **to** Roseau? (direction)
> He is the owner **of** the big pink house. (ownership)

They are very small words but they are vital to the accuracy of the message.

> Should we leave our books **on/in/under/beside/near** our desks?
> Should we make a start **before/during/after** breakfast?

CHECK YOUR UNDERSTANDING

68. Below is an extract from Chinua Achebe's *Things Fall Apart*. The prepositions have been omitted. Suggest appropriate prepositions.

    Okonkwo had just blown _____ the palm oil lamp and stretched himself _____ his bamboo bed when he heard the *ogene** _____ the town-crier piercing the still night air. *Gome, gome, gome, gome,* boomed the hollow metal. Then the crier gave his message, and _____ the end _____ it beat his instrument again. And this was his message. Every man of Umuofia was asked _____ gather _____ the market-place tomorrow morning. Okonkwo wondered what was amiss, for he knew certainly that something was amiss. He had discerned a clear overtone tragedy _____ the crier's voice, and even now he could still hear it as it grew dimmer and dimmer _____ the distance.

*ogene a musical instrument, a kind of gong

Now check your answers with the answers at the back of the book.

Using the correct preposition

Convention requires the use of specific prepositions with certain constructions.

1. Remember that the conventions of popular speech and Standard English may differ.

   Popular speech: I could stay **by** my aunt.
   Standard English: I could stay **at** my aunt's.
                                  I could stay **with** my aunt.

2. Popular speech may not require prepositions where Standard English does, and the other way round.

   Popular speech: 'You see 'e like plenty pepper? (Michael Anthony)
   Standard English: 'You can see that he likes plenty **of** pepper!'

3. If in doubt about which preposition to use after a noun, adjective or verb, consult your dictionary. You will often find just the guidance you need in the sentences given to illustrate the meaning of the word in question.

CHECK YOUR UNDERSTANDING

69. Supply appropriate prepositions. Consult your dictionary if you wish.

   a) to resort _____ violence
   b) to dispense _____ formalities
   c) to arrive _____ a decision
   d) to militate _____ our plans
   e) to revolve _____ the sun
   f) to comply _____ the regulations
   g) to gloat _____ an opponent's failure
   h) to intervene _____ a dispute
   i) to encroach _____ a friend's privacy
   j) to merge _____ the background

70. Complete these sentences with an appropriate preposition.

   a) The majority _____ the workers are happy with the offer.
   b) You have an aptitude _____ this kind of work.
   c) Parents are responsible _____ their children's behaviour.
   d) He is capable _____ great violence.
   e) A deficiency _____ Vitamin A in your diet can lead to serious problems.
   f) Ignorance _____ the law is no defence.
   g) The anxious mother asked the teacher if she was happy _____ her daughter's progress.
   h) Pearl was covered _____ confusion when she discovered she had been seen.
   i) It is difficult to cope _____ all the responsibilities of a young family.
   j) Mr Collymore hinted _____ possible changes in the firm.

71. Write sentences to show that you understand the difference in meaning that the change of preposition brings about in each of these pairs.

   a) agree to/agree with
   b) give in/give up
   c) stay with/stay up
   d) angry with/angry about
   e) look at/look into

Now check your answers with the answers at the back of the book.

Prepositions

Using the right number of prepositions

Don't skimp on prepositions.

If you are using two words or phrases in a sentence which need different prepositions, don't try to economise by using only one.

    ✘ She listened to and agreed all that he said.
    ✔ She listened **to**, and agreed **with**, all that he said.

Alternatively, recast the sentence.

    ✔ She listened **to** all that he said and agreed **with** it.

However, don't use prepositions unnecessarily.

    ✘ The dinner service comprises of sixty-four pieces.
    ✔ The dinner service comprises sixty-four pieces.
    ✘ We are planning to meet up with them in Kingston.
    ✔ We are planning to meet them in Kingston.

Consult your dictionary when in doubt.

Prepositions and personal pronouns

You will remember that pronouns have an **objective** and a **subjective** form.

    He loves foreign travel.   (subject)
    Everybody loves **him**.   (object)

Standard English requires the objective form of personal pronouns after prepositions.

Popular speech sometimes uses the subjective form and so you may have to be especially vigilant.

Popular speech: Michael said, 'Think she going come back with he?'

Standard English: Michael said, 'Do you think that she is going to come back with him?'

CHECK YOUR UNDERSTANDING

72. Choose the appropriate form of the pronoun in these sentences.

    a) The rest of _____ tried to ignore the remark. (we/us)

b) I am sure that something must have happened to _____. (he/him)
c) First my father looked at the broken windows and then he looked at _____. (we/us)
d) This must remain confidential between you and _____. (I/me)
e) With a crash, the books fell on _____. (he/him)

Now check your answers with the answers at the back of the book.

Ending a sentence with a preposition

You will frequently end sentences with a preposition in informal conversation. This is to be expected.

In formal writing, it is usually best to recast the sentence.

Informal: He is a man I hardly ever agree **with**.
Formal: He is a man **with whom** I hardly ever agree.

N.B. Be careful not to use the preposition in **both** the informal and formal positions in one sentence.

✗ He is a man **with whom** I hardly ever agree **with**.

It is not possible to recast some constructions to avoid having the preposition at the end. With others, it would result in such a clumsy, pompous construction that there is no point in doing it.

✔ What is he **like**?
✔ Whatever is this **for**?

CHECK YOUR UNDERSTANDING

73. Recast these sentences so that you avoid having the preposition at the end.

    a) Do you know which posts she has applied for?
    b) That's the bicycle I have been saving up for.
    c) I wonder which town they will choose to live in.
    d) She is the last person you ought to sympathise with.
    e) Whom is the book written by?

Now check your answers with the answers at the back of the book.

Prepositions

Conjunctions

The two types of conjunction

> He shrugged again **and** muttered, **but whether** he was talking about my morals **or** the extra work he would have to do I couldn't tell, **for** he muttered in patois.
>
> I told him to sling one of the verandah hammocks under the cedar trees **and** there I spent the rest of the day.
>
> Baptiste provided meals, **but** he seldom smiled **and** never spoke except to answer a question. My wife did not return.
>
> <div align="right">Jean Rhys, <i>Wide Sargasso Sea</i></div>

Conjunctions join. There are two types:

Co-ordinating conjunctions join parallel constructions and keep them parallel and equal.

Subordinating conjunctions join two statements by making one statement less important than the other.

Co-ordinating conjunctions

The most common co-ordinating conjunctions are 'and', 'but' and 'or'.

Co-ordinating conjunctions can join single words:

> Trinidad **and** Tobago
> tired **but** happy
> tea **or** coffee

They can join phrases:

> with great pleasure **and** with enormous pride

Co-ordinating conjunctions can also join more complicated constructions:

> Baptiste provided meals **but** he seldom smiled.

I told him to sling one of the verandah hammocks under the cedar trees **and** there I spent the rest of the day.

You will see that the three co-ordinating conjunctions have to be used very precisely.

And involves the addition of information (= plus).
But involves a contrast (= on the other hand).
Or involves an alternative (= take your pick).

CHECK YOUR UNDERSTANDING

74. Use 'and', 'but' and 'or' as appropriate to complete the gaps introduced into this extract from an article by John Gilmore in *Caribbean Week*.

There's also something known to Bajans as the Barbados cherry. Elsewhere it is simply a cherry, _____ , in the creole-speaking islands, a *cerise pays*. Botanists know the tree as *Malpighia emarginata* _____ it is not the same as the cherry familiar in temperate climates. It is indigenous to the Americas, _____ is found from Mexico to Brazil. You can suck the pulp off the three-piece stone quite easily, _____ it is a fiddly job to stone the fruit if you want them for some other purpose. They make good jam _____ fruit drinks, _____ are an excellent source of Vitamin C.
   Rather different is the Surinam cherry (*Eugenia uniflora*), a five-lobed fruit with a single round stone. It is sweet, _____ with a distinctive, almost peppery tang to it. Excellent for jam, _____ it is not easy to come by, _____ I am afraid the plants are slow-growing. Ask all your gardening friends, _____ be patient!

Now check your answers with the answers at the back of the book.

Using 'not only...but also'

Be sure to position the two halves of this conjunction very carefully.

Make sure you place them directly in front of the words to which they refer.

✔ Elsa is **not only** very intelligent, **but** she is **also** very hardworking.
✗ Elsa not only is very intelligent but she is also very hardworking.

CHECK YOUR UNDERSTANDING

75. Join these pairs of sentences using the construction 'not only...but also'. Modify the wording where necessary.

   a) He is a poet. He is also a fine dramatist.
   b) I planned to serve smoked salmon. I planned to serve roast duck.
   c) John's hair is falling out in handfuls. It is becoming very white.
   d) Debbie has visited Sweden. She has toured Holland.
   e) Merle likes table tennis. She also enjoys collecting stamps.

Now check your answers with the answers at the back of the book.

Using 'either...or' and 'neither...nor'

Take care not to mix these two constructions.

✔ You should **either** telephone him today **or** write giving full details.
✔ Jake is **neither** reliable **nor** honest.
✘ The climate is neither extremely hot in summer or very cold in winter.

CHECK YOUR UNDERSTANDING

76. Complete correctly.

   a) We can visit either Barbados _____ Bermuda this summer.
   b) The novel is neither convincing _____ well written.
   c) Either you marry me _____ you never see me again.
   d) Neither Rhonda _____ Janice is keen to organise the trip.
   e) Either hire a car when you get there _____ use mine.

Now check your answers with the answers at the back of the book.

Subordinating conjunctions

Subordinating conjunctions, as their name suggests, join statements by making one statement less important than another and dependent on it.

You are very kind. I cannot accept your offer.
Although you are very kind, I cannot accept your offer.

You see how skilfully 'although' does this job of joining and directing the reader's attention to the vital main statement 'I cannot accept your offer'.

When you first started writing essays when you were small, you probably used a great many co-ordinating conjunctions. As a more sophisticated writer, you will value the powerful elegance of subordinating conjunctions.

These are some of the most commonly used subordinating conjunctions:

after	although	as
as if	as long as	as though
because	before	even if
for	if	in case
in order that	since	so
so that	that	though
till	unless	until
when	where	whether
wherever	while	

CHECK YOUR UNDERSTANDING

77. Supply appropriate subordinating conjunctions from the list below to fill the gaps introduced into this extract from *The Friends* by Rosa Guy.

    as (once), as though (once), because (once), before (once), if (twice), that (three times), when (four times)

    Edith had not come in with the rest of the class. She never did. Teacher called her a straggler. Today _____ she straggled in from her last class I intended to surprise her. I was going to smile and make friends with her. At one time during the day I had reasoned _____ the children singled me out for abuse _____ I walked alone. They might leave me in peace _____ I walked with a friend. And so I had sat staring at the door waiting for the one girl I could use, my heart giving little leaps of delight every time someone entered, and sinking in dismay – almost down to my stomach – _____ it was not Edith.

    Soon, however, I had accepted the obvious. Edith had

carried out her earlier promise and had ducked out of school _____ the weather grew warmer. Now I wanted to leave too, panicky at the feeling of violence around me. _____ I were just to get up and go, start running, I could be far away from the school _____ class was dismissed. But gathering enough courage to simply walk out was not easy, and between the thought and the moment to act the bell rang, and the class made their dash for freedom.

A crowd was waiting for me _____ I walked down the outside steps of the school. They had gathered _____ the entire school had been given notice _____ a rumble was on. Leaving no doubt _____ I was the intended victim, a bloody roar rose _____ I appeared on the steps.

78. Complete these sentences with supporting statements beginning with the subordinating conjunction indicated.

   a) Karl dropped the parcel when _____ .
   b) I shall report you to the police unless _____ .
   c) Although _____ , I cannot forgive him.
   d) If _____ , we may be able to get tickets for Saturday's concert.
   e) As _____ , Mrs Gomez tripped and broke her leg.
   f) Did you know that _____ ?
   g) We wondered whether _____ .
   h) Alexander saved twenty dollars a week for a year so that _____ .
   i) As long as _____ , you can be sure of our support.
   j) After _____ , the burglar forced the lock.

79. Complete these sentences by using each of these subordinating conjunctions once only: whether, if, because, when, although.

   a) Hulsie deserves to pass her examinations _____ she has worked so hard.
   b) _____ she worked hard, she still did not pass.
   c) _____ only you had more confidence, you would do as well as Hulsie.
   d) _____ you decide to work harder, let me know.
   e) It is very hard to predict _____ you will pass or not.

Now check your answers with the answers at the back of the book.

CXC English Grammar

Using 'like' and 'as'

Now that we have examined both prepositions and subordinating conjunctions, you will understand why **like** and **as** cannot be used interchangeably. One is a preposition; the other is a conjunction.

Like is a preposition.

✔ She looks just **like** her father.

As is a subordinating conjunction.

✔ Roxanne washed the dishes **as** she had been told.
✔ You look **as if** you have seen a ghost.
✘ You look like you have seen a ghost.

> **CHECK YOUR UNDERSTANDING**
>
> 80. 'Like' or 'as'/'as if'?
>
>   a) You are becoming more _____ your mother every day.
>   b) _____ you would expect, he never mentioned it again.
>   c) Vincent watered the plants twice weekly _____ he had been advised.
>   d) The Prime Minister looked _____ he was going to refuse an answer.
>   e) _____ you, I have come back to St Vincent after many years away.
>
> *Now check your answers with the answers at the back of the book.*

Sentence construction

Be vigilant. Make sure when you are writing formally that you write in proper sentences, whether they are statements, commands or questions. Sentences should be grammatically self-contained, and make sense in themselves.

The construction of sentences needs care. Sloppy, unfinished sentences will certainly not impress the CXC examiners.

Which of the two examples below is a 'proper' sentence and which is only part of a sentence?

a) laughing all the way to the bank
b) he was laughing all the way to the bank

The capital letter that should begin example b) and the full stop that should end it were deliberately left out in the hope that you would recognise that it is a complete sentence without these obvious clues.

Example a) is only part of a sentence; it won't be complete until more information is added. The listener or reader is left feeling let down at the end of example a).

Example b) sounds finished, doesn't it? Grammatically this can be explained by saying that it is a statement with a subject and a verb which together make a tense.

All sentences need at least one such subject and verb.

Whether you choose to write in short, simple sentences or in more complex and varied ones will depend entirely on the context of what you are writing and the effect you are trying to achieve.

Experiment a little with sentence structures and see what advantages might be gained by breaking up long sentences into shorter ones, or by combining short sentences into more complicated structures.

There are many ways of combining a number of short statements into one smooth sentence.

I hope you will enjoy experimenting in the use of the constructions and parts of speech that we have explored during the course of this book.

The exercises should increase your verbal agility. Even more important, by flexing your verbal muscles in this way, you will acquire greater control over language and tone and emphasis. You will be better able to communicate accurately and effectively in your own writing.

See how these four statements can be combined by using different methods.

I saw Dean.
I was driving along Calcutta Street.
He disappeared down an alley.
The alley was dark and narrow.

1. I saw Dean disappear down a dark, narrow alley as I was driving along Calcutta Street.
2. Driving along Calcutta Street, I saw Dean disappear down a dark, narrow alley.
3. It was when I was driving along Calcutta Street that I saw Dean disappear down an alley that was dark and narrow.
4. Dean's disappearance down a dark and narrow alley was seen by me as I was driving along Calcutta Street.
5. The alley down which Dean disappeared while I was driving along Calcutta Street was dark and narrow.
6. I saw Dean disappearing down a dark, narrow alley while I was driving along Calcutta Street.

There will be other permutations but already we have made use of a variety of constructions:

the infinitive form:	**disappear**
abstract noun:	**disappearance**
present participle:	**driving, disappearing**
subordinating conjunctions:	**as/when/while/that**
relative pronoun:	**which**
passive voice:	**was seen**

CHECK YOUR UNDERSTANDING

81. Rewrite as three well-constructed sentences, taking care to omit none of the information given. (You may omit some words and alter constructions.) If you want to make the exercise even more challenging, you can aim to avoid using 'and', 'but' and 'or'.

    We are hoping Sophie will be starting school at Easter. Sophie is our daughter. She is four years old. I've already taught her to read. Her teacher may object. I know this. There was really no stopping her. She was fascinated by books at an early age. She would spend ages with them. She would pore over them. She would try to make sense of them. She was anxious to understand.

Conjunctions

82. Rewrite as three well-constructed sentences this recipe for barbecued red snapper.

You will need half a pound of butter, you will need 1–2 cloves of garlic. Mince the garlic. You will need the juice of one lime. Mix all these ingredients together. Set it to one side. You will need it to stuff the red snapper. Scale the red snapper. Clean the red snapper. Salt the fish inside and out. Pepper the fish inside and out. Put two tablespoonfuls of the stuffing mixture in the cavity of the fish. Barbecue the fish. Baste it with butter. Cook it for approximately ten minutes for every inch of its thickness. The remainder of the butter mixture will be useful for dipping. Serve it for this.

83. In this last exercise, recast all the information given about Frank Collymore into a well-written account, arranged in four paragraphs and not using (in total) more than seven sentences.

Frank Collymore – born 1893 – died 1980 – teacher, poet, painter, actor, editor – 'Godfather' of West Indian literature? – deserves wider recognition – edited 'Bim' for thirty years – best known for this – most important literary magazine in Caribbean under his leadership – major outlet for creative writers of region – Collymore prolific author – published seven volumes of poetry – painted some haunting water-colours – appeared in many stage productions in Barbados in leading roles – televised drama roles in later years – popular *Notes for a Glossary of Words and Phrases of Barbadian Dialect* now in sixth edition – born in Bridgetown – lived all his life in house where born – exhibition there to mark hundredth anniversary of birth – organised by Department of Archives – coincidence fiftieth anniversary of 'Bim' – special anniversary edition – Collymore's contribution to 'Bim' featured in it – present editor decided – Heinemann Educational Publishers published *The Man Who Loved Attending Funerals and Other Stories* in 1993 too – interest in centenary may lead to more informed appreciation of his work? – perhaps collected poems?

Now check your answers with the answers at the back of the book.

Answers

1. week fife father knife house segment rest pole Saturday evening dinner pig nail wood-fire holes 'bamboo' is also a noun, used here adjectivally.

2. Caribbean Trevorne Lewis St Michael's School Barbados Sunday Advocate Barbados

3. a) poverty
   b) sadness
   c) honesty
   d) length
   e) gratitude
   f) warmth
   g) energy
   h) patriotism
   i) holiness
   j) generosity

4. a) stars
   b) flowers
   c) fish
   d) small ships or boats
   e) soldiers

5. a) stitches
   b) chiefs
   c) cities
   d) radios
   e) chairs
   f) giraffes
   g) donkeys
   h) babies
   i) qualities
   j) dresses

6. a) wives
   b) mice
   c) children
   d) potatoes
   e) roofs
   f) radii
   g) brothers-in-law
   h) women
   i) shelves
   j) oxen

7. a) the workers' protests
   b) my children's toys
   c) the dog's bone
   d) the man's beard
   e) the crowd's shouts
   f) the Government's promises
   g) the dogs' growls
   h) Mr Jenkins' trousers/ Mr Jenkins's trousers
   i) their teacher's anger
   j) the examiners' comments

8. a) excitement
   b) employment, argument, statement, agreement, predicament, etc.

c) happiness, softness, harshness, weightlessness, hopelessness, etc.
d) nobility, equality, ability, generosity, equanimity, etc.
e) satisfaction, devotion, rejection, condition, caution, etc.

9. a) optimism f) pride k) sympathy p) envy
   b) cowardice g) fame l) criticism q) bravery
   c) cheerfulness h) justice m) sobriety r) cynicism
   d) extravagance i) nobility n) freedom s) loyalty
   e) beauty j) ignorance o) enthusiasm t) courage

10. a) + o)   e) + l)   i) + p)
    b) + t)   f) + s)   j) + q)
    c) + r)   g) + m)
    d) + k)   h) + n)

11. (suggestions only)
   a) Samuel
   b) Elsa, Bermuda, February
   c) Zee Edgell
   d) September
   e) Hot Socks, December

12. a) was   e) was   i) have
    b) was   f) were   j) has
    c) was   g) has
    d) was   h) have

13. a) The firemen did their best to put out the fire.
   b) I must ask you to move out.
   c) They lived happily ever after.
   d) I congratulated him on his engagement.
   e) The argument became very heated and John couldn't help losing his temper.

14. I, he, we, you, we, we, you, they, they, it

15. a) I   f) him   k) he   p) he
    b) us   g) us   l) they   q) him
    c) I   h) him   m) she   r) him
    d) they   i) she   n) us   s) we
    e) us   j) they   o) they   t) them

16. a) me   e) I   i) me
    b) I   f) me   j) me
    c) me   g) me
    d) I   h) I

CXC English Grammar

17. a) José is a friend whom I have known longer than anyone else.
b) This is the book which/that I was recommending to you yesterday.
c) We met this boy who was eighteen years old and very good-looking.
d) I was with my little nephew whom I take everywhere with me.
e) I want to find a school which/that brings out the best in each pupil.

18. a) who
b) which/that
c) whom
d) which/that
e) which/that
f) who
g) which/that
h) which/that
i) who
j) who

19. a) who
b) who
c) who
d) whom
e) who
f) who
g) who
h) who
i) whom
j) who

20. a) Aunt Grace gave my brother and me...
b) I am an only child.
d) Joyce and I are going...
e) He is always nervous.
h) I know the whole story.
i) Sam has hurt himself badly.
j) I saw myself...
l) Mollie and Thomas scratched themselves...
m) We saw the two cars crash... /We ourselves saw...
o) James and I would love to come.

c, f, g, k, n are correct.

21. a) Either: Although one...there is nothing one...
or: Although you...there is nothing you...
b) Either: One...shouldn't one?
or: You...shouldn't you?
c) Either: One...the best one can.
or: You...the best you can.
d) Either: After...one's best, one must wait...
or: After...your best, you must wait...
e) Either: It's...you dread...but you just have...as best you can.
or: It's...one dreads...but one just has...as best one can.

Answers 77

22. a) was
    b) knows
    c) is
    d) has
    e) looks

23. a) Either: A neighbour...he or she is...he or she makes.
       or: Neighbours...they...they...
    b) Either: ...the housebuyer he or she...
       or: ...the housebuyers are...they...
    c) Either: An architect...he or she admires...
       or: Architects...they...
    d) Either: A teenager...he or she deserves...
       or: Teenagers...they deserve...
    e) Either: A mother...she needs...
       or: Mothers...they need...

24. a) laughed   f) happened   k) decorated   p) pleased
    b) smiled   g) watched   l) dismissed   q) helped
    c) walked   h) listened   m) shouldered r) kicked
    d) lifted   i) fetched   n) loaded   s) packed
    e) received   j) washed   o) answered   t) confessed

25. a) advances   f) dances   k) marks   p) preaches
    b) glance   g) awards   l) delights   q) follow
    c) cope   h) play   m) hope   r) embrace
    d) practise   i) distribute   n) finishes   s) saves
    e) surprises   j) shows   o) grasps   t) believe

26. a) thought   f) hit   k) lit   p) left
    b) ran   g) agreed   l) began   q) swam
    c) told   h) put (no change) m) got   r) laid
    d) spent   i) slit (no change) n) gave   s) began
    e) led   j) swore   o) slept   t) ate

27. a) cycles
    b) have worked
    c) need
    d) loves
    e) is staying
    f) has lived
    g) apologised
    h) was hoping/hoped/had hoped
    i) do object/object
    j) was scrubbing

28. a) They come from the country and they like living in a large town.
    e) My neighbours drive new cars.
    f) When Felix saw her, he fell in love immediately.
    g) If he asked me, I wouldn't know what to say.
    i) Anna loves her little stepchildren very much and reads stories to them every night.

29. a) Her landlord says (that) she will have to move.
Her landlord says (that) she is going to have to move.
b) Will you be seeing Frank this evening?
Are you going to be seeing Frank this evening?
c) Who will mind her children?
Who is going to mind her children?
d) It will surprise my father when I tell him.
It is going to surprise my father when I tell him.
e) I shall hire a car when I get there.
I am going to hire a car when I get there.

30. a) Does Antoinette love Patrick?
b) Is she driving her father's car?
c) Don't Anthony's parents know that he is lazy?
d) Will his mother cry?
e) Do you know him well?
f) Will the shopkeepers protest at the increases?
g) Did I not tell you that I met him at the airport?
h) Are they hoping to move to St Lucia?
i) Have we failed?
j) Is she your friend?

31. a) felt...cared/feels...cares
b) would love
c) calmed...learned...was/calms...learns...is
d) kisses...collects...is/kissed...collected...was
e) called...told...thought/will call...tell...think

32. a) would leave/would be leaving/was leaving/was going to leave/had left
b) works/has worked
c) planned/was planning
d) said/was saying
e) regrets/is regretting/will regret/is going to regret

33. a) tend
b) are in need
c) was
d) were
e) don't always go

34. a) You are...
b) My sister has...
c) I am thinking...
d) If Reuben comes...
e) Have you...
f) She has...
g) Has he...

h) The children are coming...
i) He says that all his customers have gone...
j) I am hoping...

35. seek (did not seek)   do (we can do)
warn (didn't warn)   to consult
ask (did she ask)   to fix
know (do you know)   to go
say (I'll say)   wave (could wave)

36. a) He wanted to convey...
b) I heard John say...
c) She felt her heart begin...
d) I heard someone call...
e) I didn't want to talk...

37. a) to go/go   f) to catch/catch
b) to think/think   g) to be/be
c) to lay/lay   h) to fight/fight
d) to know/know   i) to swim/swim
e) to try/try   j) to feel/feel

38. a) 16   f) 2   k) 6   p) 11
b) 9   g) 14   l) 4   q) 15
c) 20   h) 10   m) 8   r) 13
d) 18   i) 12   n) 5   s) 17
e) 1   j) 7   o) 3   t) 19

39. (various possibilities)
a) Try to sort through the file quickly.../ Try to sort quickly through the file.../ Quickly try to sort through the file...
b) I've never been a person to complain endlessly...
c) The compère decided to announce the closing number immediately.
d) Simon should promise to listen carefully.../ Simon should promise to listen to professional advice carefully...
e) We want to apologise most humbly.../ We want most humbly to apologise...

40. a) risen   f) lying   k) beginning   p) replied
b) chosen   g) caught   l) laying   q) proposing
c) levelling h) agreed   m) benefited   r) beaten
d) lost   i) brought   n) sung   s) won
e) improving j) taught   o) breathing   t) bought

41. (other possibilities)
a) As she was walking home...a car...

80   CXC English Grammar

b) When he was lifting...a wasp...
   c) When they reached...the view...
   d) Everyone should enjoy ackee and saltfish if they are daintily prepared.
   e) The irate father, driven mad by infantile squabbling, sent the children to bed.

42. (other possibilities)
   a) Mr Grant told Pavana that she had fine-looking children and that they looked exactly as she had at their age.
   b) Jen told Pavana that she would be surprised at the number of things that had happened there in the week that she had been gone.
   c) Jackie Lee insisted that she loved having them all there.
   d) Pavana commented that everything about that particular job seemed to be a problem but promised that she would find a way.
   e) Pavana interrupted to tell Eric and Lisa that she would discuss it with them the next day.

43. a) All the boats in Grenada were destroyed by the hurricane.
   b) The People's Progressive Party is led by Dr Jagan.
   c) The affairs of the St Joseph Hospital have been investigated by the Public Accounts Committee.
   d) The new building has been designed by Osman, Adams and Partners.
   e) Martinique was hit by Tropical Storm Cindy on 15 August.

44. a) The town planners have completely overlooked the needs of the disabled.
   b) The pupils themselves have painted all the classrooms.
   c) His father whipped the poor child soundly.
   d) Pakistan's 'Bowler of the Year', Nadeem Khan, will lead the spin attack.
   e) Some 15 per cent of the banana growers have already abandoned land.

45. (other possibilities)
   a) Where/Why
   b) there/here
   c) elegantly/gracefully
   d) immediately/soon/quickly
   e) not
   f) very/really/terribly
   g) where
   h) sternly/kindly/angrily
   i) quite/very/extremely
   j) lazily

Answers

46. (many possibilities)
   a) scornfully/affectionately/angrily
   b) relentlessly/loudly/noisily
   c) viciously/violently/threateningly
   d) doggedly/carefully/reluctantly
   e) despairingly/comfortingly/encouragingly

47.
   a) ostentatiously
   b) aggressively
   c) vigorously
   d) apologetically
   e) pessimistically
   f) confidently
   g) ecstatically
   h) affectionately
   i) venomously
   j) chaotically

48.
   a) gently
   b) well
   c) sullenly
   d) clearly
   e) properly

49.
   a) more energetically
   b) more quickly
   c) the most neatly
   d) longer
   e) most

50. a) Nobody but the CXC candidates may queue there then.
   b) When CXC candidates are queuing there, they must not do anything else at all.
   c) CXC candidates may queue outside the General Hall but they must not queue anywhere else. (Can also mean the same as b).)
   d) CXC candidates may queue there at 10 a.m. but not at any other time. (Can also mean the same as c).)

51. a) She has no brothers or sisters.
   She is still very young.
   b) The one thing babies can do is crawl.
   Nobody but babies are able to crawl.
   c) I drink nothing but fruit juice.
   I am the only person who drinks fruit juice.
   d) You may spend five minutes with her but no longer.
   Nobody but you may see her for five minutes.

52. a) no, immediate, her
   b) government, my, school
   c) my, old, her, new, modern
   d) my, her, her, angelic
   e) her, old, her
   f) that, many, inkstained, childish
   g) my, many, far

53. (suggestions only)
   a) small, hard, sour / large, soft, sweet
   b) kind/lined/careworn
   c) hot/cruel/fierce
   d) rusty, dented/ancient/battered
   e) brown, affectionate/huge, adoring
   f) swift/sharp/vicious

58.
a) 11	e) 1	i) 5
b) 9	f) 3	j) 6
c) 2	g) 8	k) 7
d) 10	h) 4	

59.
a) cool	d) invalid	g) exorbitant
b) angry	e) boastful	h) approximate
c) rustic	f) bellicose	i) naturalistic

60.
   a) uninterested = bored
       disinterested = having no selfish motives
   b) childish = immature
       childlike = having the innocence, freshness, openness of a child
   c) catholic = universal
       Catholic = member of the Roman Catholic Church
   d) infectious = (of disease) liable to be spread by bacteria, etc. in the air, water, or on food
       contagious = (of disease) liable to be passed on easily by direct contact with people
   e) eligible = suitable, having the right qualifications
       illegible = not able to be read

61. (suggestions only)
   a) colourful, fashionable, inexpensive, clean, attractive
   b) conscientious, reliable, honest, brave, trusting
   c) loud, clear, musical, ringing, piercing
   d) untidy, large, slanted, inconsistent, spidery
   e) dark, thick, lustrous, shiny, healthy

62.
   a) circular
   b) gigantic
   c) chaotic
   d) ridiculous
   e) expensive

63. a) imaginative
b) decisive
c) moist
d) destructive
e) favourite

64. a) your supper
b) your feet
c) her mother's skirt
d) my father
e) your arm
f) our side
g) my firm ambition
h) her arms
i) his house
j) your vote

65. (suggestions only)
a) For sale: vacuum cleaner, complete with new hose and dustbag. Recently overhauled by mechanic.
b) My mother decided sadly that her arthritic and incontinent sixteen-year-old retriever should be put to sleep.
c) Mrs Kelly visited her mother, who was very lonely OR Mrs Kelly, who was very lonely, visited her mother.
d) I gave the pupil the safety-pins I always keep in my handbag.
e) For the children she bought bicycles with chrome fittings.

66. a) most beautiful
b) taller
e) at a faster pace
f) you would be happier
h) one of the noisiest villages

67. a) fewer
b) fewer
c) less
d) less
e) fewer

68. These are the prepositions that Chinua Achebe used:
(blown) out
(stretched himself) on
(ogene) of
at (the end) of (it)
to (gather) at (the market-place)
(overtone) of (tragedy) in
in (the distance)

69. a) to
b) with
c) at
d) against
e) around, round
f) with
g) over
h) in
i) upon/on
j) into

70. a) of
b) for
c) for
d) of
e) in/of
f) of
g) with
h) in
i) with
j) at

71. (suggestions)

a) Reluctantly we agreed to accept whatever changes were necessary.
(i.e. We gave our consent.)
I agree with you entirely.
(i.e. I have the same opinion as you.)
b) I give in. Tell me the answer.
(i.e. I have been defeated.)
Robert is giving up sarcastic remarks for Lent.
(i.e. Robert will stop being sarcastic for 40 days.)
c) Mrs Kincaid is very distressed. Will you stay with her?
(i.e. keep her company)
My mother always stays up until I get home.
(i.e. doesn't go to bed)
d) Mr Cresswell is angry about the damage caused and is angry with you for causing it.
(One is angry **about** things or happenings and angry **with** people.)
e) Look at the two photographs very carefully.
(i.e. Use your eyes.)
The police are looking into the matter.
(i.e. investigating)

72. a) us
b) him
c) us
d) me
e) him

73. a) Do you know for which posts she has applied?
b) That's the bicycle for which I have been saving up.
c) I wonder in which town they will choose to live.
d) She is the last person with whom you ought to sympathise.
e) By whom is the book written?

Answers

74. The conjunctions used in the *Caribbean Week* article are:
or (in creole-speaking islands)   and (are an excellent source)
and (it is not the same)   but (with a distinctive)
and (is found)   but (it is not easy)
but (it is a fiddly job)   and (I am afraid)
or (fruit drinks)   and (be patient)

75. a) He is not only a poet but also a fine dramatist.
    b) I planned to serve not only smoked salmon but also roast duck.
    c) John's hair is not only falling out in handfuls but it is also becoming very white.
    d) Debbie has not only visited Sweden but she has also toured Holland.
    e) Merle not only likes table tennis but she also enjoys collecting stamps.

76. a) or   d) nor
    b) nor   e) or
    c) or

77. These are the prepositions Rosa Guy used:
when (she straggled)   before (class)
that (the children)   when (I walked)
because (I walked)   as though (the entire school)
if (I walked)   that (a rumble)
when (it was not)   that (I was)
as (the weather)   when (I appeared)
If (I were)

78. (suggestions only)
    a) when I arrived
    b) unless you return the stolen goods
    c) Although I still love him
    d) If we telephone immediately
    e) As she was leaving our house
    f) that Albert and Rita are getting married
    g) whether you would sponsor us
    h) so that he could buy a racing bicycle
    i) As long as you do your best
    j) After he had tried every other means of entry

79. a) because   d) when
    b) although   e) whether
    c) if

80. a) like
b) as
c) as
d) as if
e) like

81. (suggestion)
We are hoping that Sophie, our four-year-old daughter, will be starting school at Easter. I know that her teacher may object because I've already taught her to read but there was really no stopping her. Fascinated by books at an early age, she would pore over them, trying to make sense of them and anxious to understand.

82. (suggestion)
Make the stuffing by mixing together half a pound of butter, 1–2 cloves of garlic (minced) and the juice of one lime, and set to one side. After cleaning the red snapper and seasoning it with salt and pepper inside and out, stuff the cavity of the fish with two tablespoonfuls of the stuffing and barbecue, basting with butter and allowing ten minutes cooking time for every inch of the fish's thickness. Serve with the remainder of the butter for dipping.

83. (suggestion)
Frank Collymore (1893–1980), teacher poet, painter, actor, author, and editor (and many would say the godfather of West Indian literature) has yet to receive the wider recognition that he so richly deserves.

Best known for his thirty-year editorship of 'Bim', which became under his leadership the most important literary magazine in the English-speaking Caribbean and a major outlet for the region's creative writers, he was also a painter of haunting water-colours, a leading actor in many Barbadian stage productions (appearing in televised drama in his later years) and a prolific author, publishing seven volumes of poetry. His popular *Notes for a Glossary of Words and Phrases of the Barbadian Dialect* is now in its sixth edition.

To mark the centenary of his birth, the Department of Archives mounted a fascinating exhibition at his birthplace and lifelong home in Bridgetown. By happy coincidence it was also the fiftieth anniversary of 'Bim' and its present editor celebrated Collymore's contribution to the magazine in a special anniversary issue. Happily also, Heinemann

Educational Publishers published in his centenary year *The Man Who Loved Attending Funerals and Other Stories*.

We can only hope that the interest shown at the centenary will lead to a more informed appreciation of his work and indeed to a collected edition of his poetry.

use 42–3
passive voice 45–7
past/present tense 24, 25–30
personal pronouns 12, 13–16, 57, 64–5
plurals
   collective nouns 8–10
   fewer & *less*, using 60
   spelling of nouns 2–4
popular speech
   and adverbs 50
   could of/could have 35–6
   emphasis 30
   and possessive 4, 5
   and prepositions 62
   and pronouns 14–15, 57, 64
   questions 33
   tenses 24, 31
possessive
   adjectives 53, 57
   apostrophe 4–5
   pronouns 12
prepositions
   definition 61
   ending sentences 65
   and infinitives 37
   like & *as* 71
   and personal pronouns 64–5
   right number of 64
   using correct 62–3
present/past tense 24, 25–30
pronouns
   demonstrative 12
   emphasising 12, 19–21
   indefinite 12, 21–2
   interrogative 12, 19
   matching nouns 23
   personal 12, 13–16, 57, 64–5
   possessive 12
   reflexive 12, 19–21
   relative 12, 17–18
   types of 12
proper
   adjectives 54
   nouns 1–2, 7–8
punctuation: proper nouns 7–8

questions, formation of 32–3

reflexive pronouns 12, 19–21
relative
   adjectives 53–4
   adverbs 48, 49
   pronouns 12, 17–18

sentences
   clarity/simplicity 10–11
   construction 71–4
   and prepositions 61, 65
sequence of tenses 34–6
should have, using 35–6
speech *see* direct speech; indirect speech; popular speech
spelling
   participles 42
   plural nouns 2–4
split infinitives 40–1
style
   clarity & simplicity 10–11
   and sentence construction 71–4
subjects
   active & passive voice 45–6
   matching verbs 36–7
   personal pronouns as 13, 15–16, 64
subordinating conjunctions 66, 68–71
superlative
   adjectives 59–60
   adverbs 50–1

tenses
   future 31–2
   and participles 42
   present/past 24, 25–30
   sequence of 34–6

verbs
   active/passive voice 45–7
   and collective nouns 8–10
   definition 24
   direct/indirect speech 44–5
   emphatic/simple forms 28, 29, 30–1
   formation of questions 32–3
   and indefinite pronouns 22
   infinitives 37–41
   irregular 26–8
   matching subjects 36–7
   negatives 33–4
   participles 42–4
   tenses
      future 31–2
      present/past 24, 25–30
      sequence of 34–6
vocabulary 6

who & *whom*, using 17, 18, 19
would have, using 35–6

you & *one*, using 21–2

Index

abstract nouns 1, 2, 6–7
active voice 45–7
adjectives 53–60
    comparison 59–60
    demonstrative 53
    emphasising 54
    exclamatory 54
    fewer & *less* 60
    interrogative 53
    participles 42, 43
    positioning 57–8
    possessive 53, 57
    proper 54
    of quality 53
    of quantity 53
    relative 53–4
    types 53–4
adverbs
    comparison of 50–1
    of degree 48, 49
    interrogative 48
    of manner 48, 49
    negatives 48, 49, 51
    of place 48, 49
    and popular speech 50
    positioning of *only* 52
    relative 48, 49
    of time 48, 49
    types 48–50
agreement
    collective nouns and verbs 8–10
    pronouns and nouns 23
    subject & verb 36–7
apostrophe, possessive 4–5
as & *like*, using 71

capital letters 7–8
class terms 9–10
co-ordinating conjunctions 66–8
collective nouns 1, 2, 8–10
common nouns 1
comparative
    adjectives 59–60
    adverbs 50–1
conjunctions
    co-ordinating 66–8
    subordinating 66, 68–71
could of & *could have*, using 35–6

demonstrative
    adjectives 53
    pronouns 12
direct speech 44–5

either ... or, using 68
emphasis
    and adjectives 54
    and pronouns 12, 19–21
    verbs 28, 29, 30–1
everyone/everybody/everything, using 22
exclamatory adjectives 54

fewer & *less*, using 60
future tense 31–2

indefinite pronouns 12, 21–2
indirect speech 44–5
infinitives 37–41
interrogative
    adjectives 53
    adverbs 48
    pronouns 12, 19
irregular verbs 26–8

less & *fewer*, using 60
like & *as*, using 71

negatives
    and adverbs 48, 49, 51
    formation of 33–4
neither ... nor, using 68
not only ... but also, using 67–8
nouns
    abstract 1, 2, 6–7
    adjectival 54
    collective 1, 2, 8–10
    common 1
    matching pronouns 23
    plurals 2–4, 8–10, 60
    possessive apostrophe 4–5
    proper 1–2, 7–8

objects, personal pronouns as 13–14, 15–16, 64
one & *you*, using 21–2
only, positioning of 52

participles
    misrelated 43–4